SHIPS THAT SHAPED
AUSTRALIA

Written and illustrated by Jack L. Koskie

Foreword by Geoffrey Blainey

To Jim & Moira,
with best wishes
& thanks for your
kind hospitality
Jack L. Koskie

ANGUS
& ROBERTSON
PUBLISHERS

Dedicated to my wife, Hanna,
for her valued assistance and encouragement

ANGUS & ROBERTSON PUBLISHERS

Unit 4, Eden Park, 31 Waterloo Road,
North Ryde, NSW, Australia 2113, and
16 Golden Square, London WIR 4BN,
United Kingdom

First published in Australia
by Angus & Robertson Publishers in 1987

Copyright © J. L. Koskie, 1987

National Library of Australia
Cataloguing-in-publication data.

Koskie, Jack, 1914-   .
  Ships that shaped Australia.
  ISBN 0 207 15560 7.

  1. Ships—Australia—History. 2. Australia—History.
  I. Title.
387.2'0994

Typeset in Bembo by Midland Typesetters
Printed in Singapore

Contents

Foreword

In that long era when much of Australia's history was shaped by the sea, thousands of ships ranging from ketches to four-funnel liners called at Australian ports. Most had vanished or had become hulks or wrecks by the time the coloured film and photograph arrived. A few of the famous ships can be seen in coloured lithographs, black-and-white sketches, postcards or illuminated addresses. Occasionally for historical films a celebrated sailing ship has been re-erected, as it were, on the sea and filmed with a flair and cunning that partly conceals the historical inaccuracies. It is a form of historical piracy but enough to satisfy us as we watch the television.

When you look at these painted ships with white sails billowing or funnels puffing black smoke, you see not only the majesty of sky and ocean but an important fragment of the lost past. This is the first serious attempt to paint many of these ships, painting them not as we imagine them but as they were. The result is captivating.

Jack Koskie, the author of this book, was born in Hull, Yorkshire, in 1914 and first went to sea in an Iceland-bound trawler at the age of sixteen. Away for some five weeks, catching cod and haddock and halibut, Jack was a kind of marine rouseabout—a "decky learner"— who spent much of the day handing wooden boxes to the men gutting the fish and packing them. Later he studied both art and printing before emigrating to Australia, which he reached on the day the Second World War broke out. After serving in the merchant navy and then in the army as camouflage designer, he became a publisher's designer and illustrator, the head of the department of graphic design and print making at the Hobart Technical College and the senior art master at Mount Scopus College near Melbourne, finishing his teaching career in 1979 as lecturer in print making at Deakin University. Meanwhile he painted oils and watercolours and made prints and lithographs; and his work is now in many Australian galleries.

Conceiving a series of paintings of thirty or forty significant Australian ships, Jack Koskie did not realise how long he would spend merely trying to find the elementary details without which no historical painting could be accurate. He tried to ascertain the weather on the day a certain ship entered a harbour for the first time, and also the direction of the wind, the colour and mood of the sea and the exact sails the ship was carrying. He felt a need to visit harbours to capture the light and landscape: thus he visited Kangaroo Point in Brisbane to sketch the cliffs before depicting the *Rose* passing the Point. When he sought the details of certain ships—their rigging, the colour of their hull or the size of their masts—he found the weightiest authorities could contradict each other. When in doubt, Jack Koskie told me, "I made no statement at all in a painting—unless absolutely forced to." In selecting ships and their masters, he liked especially what he calls the "little blokes".

With his brush and pen he is very much the practical sailor, telling us what could and could not happen in the inflexible era of sail. Thus he explains how the sailing ship *Loch Ard*, approaching a sea fog in the rugged coast east of Warrnambool (Victoria), was already too close to land when at four in the morning the lookout shouted his warning. There was no space or time to make the manoeuvre necessary to turn a large ship. A steamship might have reversed and escaped but the sailing ship was trapped.

To the early settlers of Australia a ship had a magic and importance which we cannot quite imagine, for she brought them news and supplies from home, and when they were tired of Australia, she carried them away. Barron Field, the first judge of the Supreme Court in infant Sydney, summed up this longing when in 1819 he wrote in the first volume of verse to be published in this land that "a ship's the only poetry we see". Jack Koskie captures, in generation after generation of ships, something of that poetry.

GEOFFREY BLAINEY

1

Preface

Australia made its appearance slowly and painfully on the map of the world: its outline was defined bit by bit. Spanish, Portuguese, Dutch, French and British seamen made their mark. Names of seamen such as Torres, Tasman, Dampier, La Pérouse and others in their tiny ships, but most of all, those of Cook and Flinders, are amply perpetuated on our charts and sometimes in our history books. They are "establishment" names, familiar to most Australians.

Of the men who followed and did the ground work for our growth, the convicts and early migrants, much has been written—many dramas and many romances. They all came by sea and by sail, until steam and diesel made light of the hazards of the voyage from distant Europe. Not many people today can name a single ship of this exciting period, and even fewer can distinguish a ship of 1835 from one of 1885, although these dates span a period which witnessed the greatest change in travel until the advent of the aeroplane.

Even less known are those early seamen, whalers and settlers—together with the many types of ships they employed—who took part in the founding and development of our coastal towns and those along the Murray and other rivers, long before the roads and railways reached out to fill the spaces in between. Their part is only known to a few; their ships were hardly spectacular; and their efforts in the enrichment and growth of Australia are poorly recorded and seem quite unappreciated.

The aim of this book is to commemorate in word and picture those men and their ships, and to indicate their part in the shaping and making of Australia. To accomplish this with accuracy, and in a manner easily accessible to a wide audience, has been quite a task.

It has involved years of research, sometimes frustrating but often exciting; reliable documentation is scarce.

I discovered my most inspirational document in London's British Museum. It was written by Dominic Serres and his son John and was published in 1805. Dominic was a French seaman who was captured by the British and settled in England, becoming a founding member of the Royal Academy and its first librarian. Their words follow:

Address to the Amateurs of Marine Painting

The numerous applications for rudiments to acquire a knowledge of the drawing of Shipping and Ships, will I hope be sufficient excuse for introducing the work to the notice of the Public; although I am well convinced, notwithstanding the intricacy of the subject, it may from the manner in which the principles of The Arts are exposed, be found in some degree serviceable and more explanatory than any plan of a similar kind which has hitherto been produced.

Many are the obstacles to the attainment of Drawing Marine Subjects particularly as it is not only requisite that a person Desirous of excelling in this Art should possess a knowledge of the construction of a Ship or what is Denominated "Naval Architecture" together with the proportion of masts and yards, the Width, Depth and cut of the sails, etc., but he should likewise be acquainted with Seamanship.

The important objects will Doubtless be much promoted by the present Publication, the plan and execution of which, will, I hope convey a general accurate idea of a Ship and its Component Parts, even to such as are unacquainted with the floating monuments of British Power. The 2nd part of this work which was designed by my Father will be found to contain specimens of all the different kinds of Ships and Vessels, which are made still further interesting and amusing by the introduction in the background, of scenes taken from nature and characteristic of the ships.

This publication when completed will form a handsome Literary Volume. The Method of Drawing being so easy and so generally understood, it is unnecessary to make any remarks in illustration of the subject, the process being the same in this as in every other branch of the arts. J. Serres

3

Liber Nauticus and instructor in
the ART OF MARINE PAINTING.

....

By Dominic Serres R.A.
&
John Thomas Serres

Marine Painter to His Majesty, His Royal Highness the Duke
of Clarence
and Marine draughtsman to the Honour-Board of the Admiralty.

....

Published & Sold by Edward Orme,
His Majesty's Printseller,
559 Bond St. London. 1805.
Printed by John Nichols,
Earls Court, Newport St. Soho.

To "knowledge of ships and seamanship" must be added a feeling for the oneness of ships, sea and sky and the mood this conveys. The *Address* was accompanied by a collection of engravings and aquatints showing the types of craft of the times. They are set in the waters of England and Europe, the Thames and the North Sea.

Ships That Shaped Australia is an Australian book. All except two of the paintings depict ships in Australian waters, with mostly blue skies. I have tried to show the breeze, warm or cold, how a ship sits in the water, how wave shapes vary according to the form of the hull, the tides and currents, and differences in wave patterns between inshore and open seas. Where appropriate I have also tried to indicate a specific locality in the hope that Victorians may recognise their own Port Phillip Bay, Sydneysiders their harbour, Queenslanders their Brisbane River and so on right around Australia. Local pride must be respected.

To portray ships as the travellers of the day saw them, with as many temperamental variants as human beings, has also been my aim. I have tried to ascertain which were awkward ships, which were hated or loved by passengers and crew — as much as could be gleaned from log books, letters home, contemporary newspapers and many other sources.

For help with this I wish to thank the National Library in Canberra, the specialist State Libraries — the Mitchell Library in Sydney, John Oxley Library in Brisbane, Battye Library in Perth and La Trobe Library, Melbourne — also the Baillieu Library of Melbourne University, Adelaide University Library and History Department, Deakin University Library, Geelong, the Tasmanian Archives and Library, Hobart, and even the suburban Moorabbin Municipal Library. Thanks also to the shipping companies, Burns Philp and McIlwraith McEacharn.

Research has taken me to the National Maritime Museum, Greenwich, and to maritime museums in Liverpool, Hull, Portsmouth, Plymouth and other sea ports in the UK as well as Fremantle Maritime Museum, Albany Museum and other Australian museums.

I have enjoyed assistance from the Maritime Museum at Salem, Massachusetts, USA, the World Ship Society and the Australian Association for Maritime History. I also acknowledge the research grant from the Literature Board of the Australia Council and Ansett Airways for their assistance with travel to Brisbane and Sydney. To all these I express my thanks.

The sepia ink of the shipping clerk's quill is fast fading. The ship masters' logs recording the events of the voyage and newspaper reports of the day must be read with special understanding. But all this bonded with material and advice from many sources provides a sound anchorage for the facts. These I have not romanticised. Where dimensions and other statistics are given, they are in the terms and measurement systems of the day and come mostly from Lloyd's Register.

The "little ships" and their great men seem to have been swallowed up by history and their story, like the ink of the nineteenth century, is fading. However, ultimately my most difficult task has been to decide which ship to include. Every ship developed its own personality and "did its bit" in shaping modern Australia.
                                                                    J. L. KOSKIE

Glossary

The sailors' vocabulary contains many marvellous words and terms. This glossary records not only those relevant to this book but those most commonly in use today.

ABACK A square rigger is taken aback if the wind is allowed, inadvertently, to come front on to the sails.

ABAFT In or towards the stern.

ABOUT To turn across the wind. A ship is going about when turning to bring the wind on the other side of the sails.

AFT At or near the stern.

ASTERN In, at or towards the rear of a vessel, or in a backwards direction.

ATHWART From side to side across a ship. The seats in a rowing boat are called thwarts.

BAR-BOAT A small shallow boat built for negotiating sand-covered entrances to river mouths.

BARQUE A sailing vessel, usually three-masted—square-rigged on the first and second masts (foremast and mainmast) and fore and aft rigged on the third mast (the mizzen) (see *Sail Rigging* diagram).

BARQUENTINE Similar to a barque but square-rigged on the first or foremast only (see *Sail Rigging* diagram).

BEAM The measurement of a ship at its widest part.

BOOM The long horizontal spar at the base of a fore and aft sail (see *Sail Types* diagram).

BOW The front of a ship. The various forms of bow are: clipper, fiddle, straight stem and bulbous, the last being seen on large modern cargo ships.

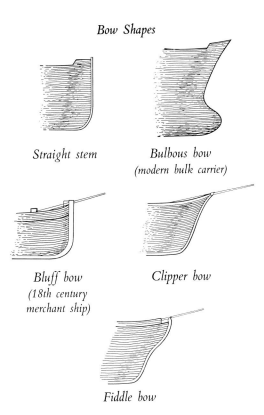

Bow Shapes

Straight stem

Bulbous bow (modern bulk carrier)

Bluff bow (18th century merchant ship)

Clipper bow

Fiddle bow

BOWSPRIT The long spar projecting forward over the bow of a sailing ship, mainly to take the stays holding the mast forward.

BRIG A sailing ship with two square-rigged masts (see *Sail Rigging* diagram).

BRIGANTINE Similar to a brig but square-rigged on the first or foremast only (see *Sail Rigging* diagram).

BROACH TO An uncontrolled turn from a following wind, side on to the wind. This turns a ship from sailing across waves and troughs to a broadside position which, in a heavy sea, could lead to its being swamped or capsized.

BULBOUS BOW See "Bow".

BULWARK A wall protecting the decks of a ship.

BUNKER Compartment for storage of coal or other fuel.

BURTHEN A vessel's carrying capacity originally related to barrels of wine.

CARRACK A large type of trading vessel of the fourteenth to seventeenth centuries.

CARVEL BUILT A method of construction of a wooden ship, in which the timber planking of the hull is laid edge to edge.

CLINKER BUILT A method of construction of a wooden ship, in which the timber planking of the hull is overlapped.

Hull Construction
Methods of fixing planking to hull framing

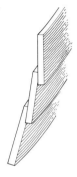 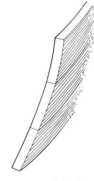

Clinker built   *Carvel built*

CLIPPER BOW See "Bow".

CLOSE HAULED Sails are tightly braced or "sheeted in" so that their curve is flattened as close as possible—the procedure employed when sailing close to the wind.

COMPOUND ENGINE A development from the single-cylinder to twin-cylinder steam engine. After steam has expanded in a smaller high pressure cylinder, it passes into a second, larger cylinder to expand again, adding to the engine power.

CORVETTE A flush-decked warship of the eighteenth century, smaller than a frigate but with similar rig. This name was used for a class of fast escort vessel used in World War Two.

COUNTER The section of a stern overhanging the rudder post (see *Sterns* diagram).

COUNTER STERN See "Stern".

CRUISER STERN See "Stern".

CUTTER RIG A single mast with four sails set two fore, both jibs, and two aft, a mainsail and topsail (see *Sail Rigging* diagram).

DAVITS Small cranes for lowering ships' boats.

DERRICK A long spar fixed at its lower end to the bottom mast and used for working cargo.

EASE, TO Taking the pressure out of a sail by easing the ropes or sheets.

EYE OF THE WIND A term describing the direction from which the wind blows.

FIDDLE BOW See "Bow".

FLUSH DECK A continuous deck running from bow to stern.

FLUTE An eighteenth century Dutch supply ship with three masts, characterised by round lines and poop deck.

FORE AND AFT RIG Sails hung in the direction of the length of a ship in front of and behind the mast.

FORE AND AFT SAIL A sail that hangs along the length of a vessel rather than across it as in a square rigger (see *Sail Types* diagram).

FORECASTLE, FO'C'SLE Originally, in the thirteenth and fourteenth centuries, this was a fighting platform built over the bow. In later warships it was a small raised platform for obser-vation and command under which the seamen were quartered. Today the fighting platform is no more but the term remains in use to describe the seamen's quarters or the forward part of a vessel.

FOREMAST The first mast behind the bow.

FOTHER A method of stopping a leak while a ship is at sea, by pulling a sail outside and around the hull to cover the damage. The water pressure blocks the damaged area.

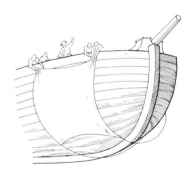

Fothering a damaged hull

FREE Sailing free with eased sail ropes or sheets, and the wind from astern (see *General Principles of Sailing* diagram).

FREEBOARD The distance from the waterline to the upper-deck level of a ship.

FRIGATE An eighteenth century class of full-rigged ship, armed with twenty-four to thirty guns on one deck. Faster and more manoeuvrable than "ships of the line". Their main function was to act as lookout and messenger ships.

GAFF A spar holding out the head of a four-sided fore and aft sail (see *Sail Types* diagram).

GALLIOT A small Dutch trading ship, generally single-masted. Bluff, rounded lines and very good sea boats.

GUNWALE, GUNNEL The upper edge of the side of a vessel used formerly to support guns.

HALYARD A rope, wire and tackle for hoisting and lowering sails or flags.

HATCH An opening in the deck of a ship for access to the holds.

HEADSAIL A sail set before the mast. Also know as a jib or, when set on a stay, a staysail.

HOVE TO Stopping a ship in sail at sea. As a rule, accomplished by backing, that is, setting some of the sail area to take the wind front on.

HULL The main body of the ship, not including masts and sails.

IN STAYS A sailing ship is "in stays" when head on into the wind and unable to move on to either tack.

JACKYARD TOPSAIL A triangular sail set between mast and gaff and extended by a jackyard (see *Cutter Rig* diagram).

JIBHEADED TOPSAIL A sail filling the triangle between gaff and mast, sometimes called leg o'mutton topsail.

KEEL The spine of a ship running centrally along the length of its bottom. The keel is the longest structural member of a ship's frame.

KETCH A two masted fore and aft rigged sailing ship, the second mast shorter than the foremast (see *Sail Rigging* diagram).

KNOT A unit of speed at sea, being one nautical mile per hour.

LATEEN SAIL

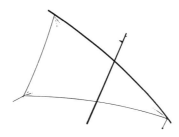

Used by the Portuguese and Dutch during the 15th and 17th centuries.

LINER A ship carrying passengers on a scheduled route.

LIST The inclining of a ship to one side, due to cargo shift or damage.

LLOYD'S OF LONDON An association of merchants and insurance underwriters. The name is from a coffee house in London where the merchants met in 1601.

LLOYD'S REGISTER In 1760 Lloyd's drew up a set of rules regarding the construction of ships for the protection of its underwriters. The Register listed all ships built to those rules and rated them accordingly. A1 at Lloyd's is top classification.

LOG BOOK A document kept on board ship to record information about navigation and working of a ship.

LOOSE FOOT A fore and aft sail set without a boom (see *Sail Types* diagram).

LUGGER A small sailing vessel setting lugsail (see diagram).

LUGSAIL

Used on small craft such as fishing boats.

MAINMAST The second mast behind the bow.

MAINSAIL The biggest sail on a vessel. On a sloop the mainsail is set behind the mast and reaches to its head.

MILE, NAUTICAL A measure of

distance at sea which is equal to 1853 metres.

MIZZEN   The third mast after the bow.

OFF THE WIND   Sailing to catch the following wind with sails eased off as far as possible.

ON THE WIND   Sailing as close to the wind as possible with the sails "sheeted in" (see *General Principles of Sailing* diagram).

PACKET BOAT   An early name for small ships on a scheduled route between two or three ports. The term preceded that of "liner".

PAY OFF   To close the account of a ship on completion of a commission. Also, to turn away from the wind.

PEAK   The upper corner of a fore and aft sail (see *Sail Types* diagram).

POOP   A short deck over the stern of a ship.

POOPED   A ship is pooped when a heavy following sea breaks over the stern, reducing the grip of the rudder.

PORT   The left side of a ship when facing forward from the stern.

PORT TACK   Sailing with the wind on the port side (see *General Principles of Sailing* diagram).

QUARTER   The after sides of a ship, from midships to stern.

RATLINES   The small lines of rope across the shrouds of a ship forming a ladder.

READY ABOUT   The order given preparatory to tacking, or going about.

REEF POINTS   A row of short ropes attached along the base of a sail to allow it to be rolled and tied and thus expose less surface to the wind.

REEFING   The operation of shortening a sail by rolling and tying it along the reef points.

RUNNING THE EASTING DOWN   Sailing from west to east in the latitudes 40 to 50 degrees south, the "Roaring Forties". Sailing ships to Australia used this route to take advantage of the prevailing westerly gales.

SCANTLING   Originally, finished dimensions of ships' timbers in the construction of the hull. Some rules for this published in Lloyd's Register.

SCHOONER   Usually a two masted fore and aft rigged sailing ship, when the main mast, the second mast, is equal to or taller than the fore mast (see *Sail Rigging* diagram).

SCUPPERS   Drainage openings in the bulwarks and the gutter, to allow water to run over the side.

SHEETED IN   See "close hauled".

SHEETS   Ropes that are part of the running rigging, controlling the set of the sails.

SHROUDS   The standing rigging which supports a mast laterally, across the beam, athwart ships.

SLOOP   Used throughout history generally to describe a small, fast sailing ship. Nowadays it describes a yacht with one fore sail and one main sail on one mast.

Modern sloop, Bermudian rig.

SNOW   A brig rigged ship i.e. square sails on both masts but with a small trysail mast stepped immediately abaft the main mast.

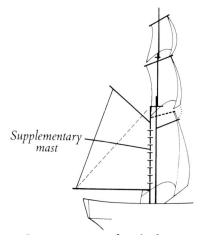

Quarter view or aft end of Snow showing supplementary mast arrangement.
The dotted line shows an alternative trisail.

SOLDIER'S WIND   An easy wind blowing steadily on the beam of a sailing ship, which makes tacking unnecessary on a long leg. It requires very little skill from the helmsman.

SPANKER A fore and aft sail set on the after side of the last (or mizzen) mast.

SPINNAKER A large balooning triangular foresail on a light boom that can be raised for extra speed when running before the wind.

SPONSON A platform on the outside of a ship's hull. In a paddle steamer, that structure projecting forward and aft of the paddle boxes.

SPRITSAIL A fore and aft sail set on a sprit or a spar attached to the outer top corner of a sail and fastened to the base of a mast. Used mainly on small sailing ships.

*Used on small European craft.
The Thames barges still use this rig.*

STARBOARD The right side of a ship, when facing forward from the stern.

STARBOARD TACK Sailing with the wind on the starboard side (see *General Principles of Sailing* diagram).

STAYS The standing rigging which supports a mast longitudinally, fore and aft, on which sails are sometimes set.

STAYSAIL A sail set on stays. This can be before the mast, as on sloops, or between the masts, as on square-rigged ships.

STEERAGE Large space below decks, often just above the propellors. This was used in the nineteenth and early twentieth centuries, to provide dormitory-type accommodation for emigrant passengers unable to pay for a cabin.

STEERAGE WAY Sufficient speed ahead to allow the rudder to grip the water and the ship to be steered or "to answer the helm".

STERN The after end of the ship. Basic forms are tuck, reverse tuck, transom, counter and cruiser.

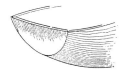 

Tuck stern with counter   *Reverse tuck stern
(modern racing yacht)*

Counter stern   *Cruiser stern*

Transom stern   *Transom stern
(modern bulk carrier)*

STRAIGHT STEM See "Bow".

THWARTS The seats in a rowing boat which run from side to side across the hull.

TONNAGE Originally tunnage, the tax levied in 1347 by Edward III of England on one tun barrel of imported wine. There are various measurements of tonnage but merchant ships are usually quoted on hold capacity or gross tonnage, a unit being approximately 100 cubic feet. The new metric tonne system is close enough to the old ton to cause little confusion among old hands.

TRANSOM STERN See "Stern"

TRIPLE EXPANSION ENGINE An 1870 to 1880 development of the compound engine (q.v.). By the addition of a third and larger cylinder the steam expands a third time, further increasing power.

TRISAIL A three-cornered sail (see *Snow* diagram).

TUCK STERN See "Stern".

WHERRY A single deck sailing vessel of very shallow draught, used for transport of small quantities of freight on rivers or canals.

YAWING An involuntary deviation off course, in sail.

YAWL A two masted fore and aft rigged sailing ship with the second mast shorter and stepped abaft the rudder.

Sail and Sail Rigging

1. Spanker.
2. Mizzen royal.
3. Topgallant:
   sometimes, especially on larger ships, divided into upper and lower topgallant.
4. Mizzen topsail:
   sometimes divided into upper and lower topsail.

5. Mizzen course.
6. Main royal.
7. Main topgallant:
   sometimes divided into upper and lower topgallant.
8. Main topsail:
   sometimes divided into upper and lower topsail.

9. Main course.
10. Fore royal.
11. Fore topgallant:
    sometimes divided into upper and lower topgallant.
12. Fore topsail:
    sometimes divided into upper and lower topsail.

13. Fore course.
14. Foresails or jibs.
15. Shrouds and stays to hold up the mast.
    Fore stays leading from fore mast to bowsprit hold the mast forward.
16. Bowsprit.

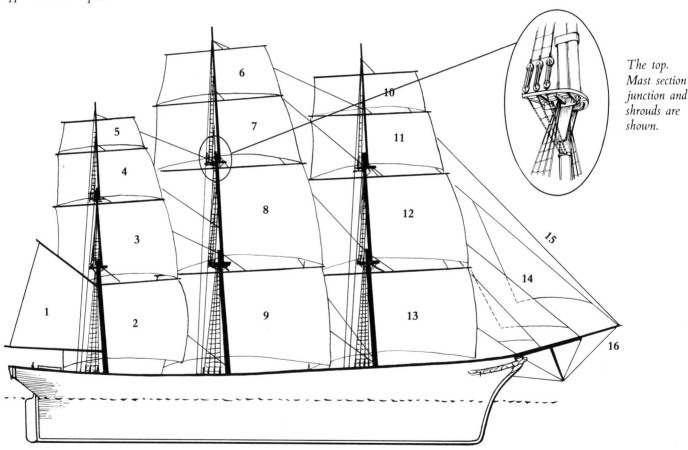

The top. Mast section junction and shrouds are shown.

The full rigged ship

The diagram shows the main working sail areas of a full rigged ship of the clipper type. The standing rigging consists of the shrouds and stays that hold up the masts. The running rigging, that operates the setting and movement of the sails, is not shown as it would amount to a maze of over one hundred lines.

The various sail rigs of ships that worked along the Australian coast.

BARQUE   BARQUENTINE   BRIG   BRIGANTINE   TOPSAIL SCHOONER   KETCH   CUTTER

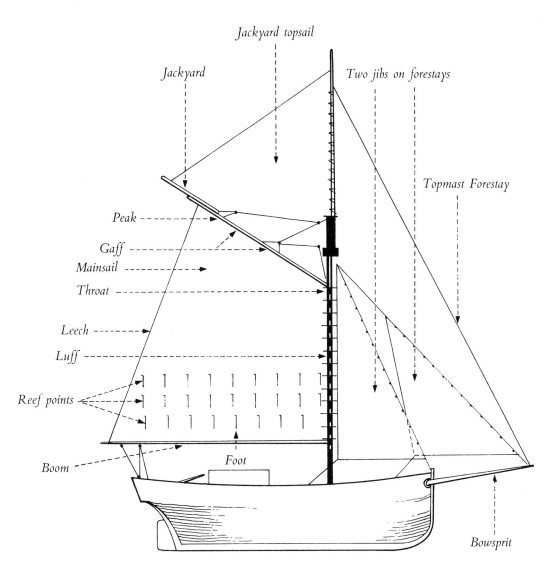

Jackyard topsail

Jackyard

Two jibs on forestays

Topmast Forestay

Peak

Gaff

Mainsail

Throat

Leech

Luff

Reef points

Boom

Foot

Bowsprit

Cutter Rig

A rig of the mid 19th century showing points of the mainsail. A jackyard topsail is shown here but topsails varied on these craft.

11

General Principles of Sailing

The diagram shows a barque at three stages of going about:

On port tack.

On starboard tack.

Going about, the barque's square sails momentarily aback and pressing
against the mast. It is a manoeuvre requiring skilful timing. This small
waterline sketch shows the sails on the main mast aback, the middle of the action.

The diagram on the opposite page describes the action of the fore and aft rig, the sails swinging over automatically.
The square rig involves the same principle, but the manoeuvre is more complicated, requiring more time and sea room. The yards and sails are
manually hauled and braced to meet the new tack and get the wind behind the sails in rotation. The ship must keep enough
momentum to allow for this.

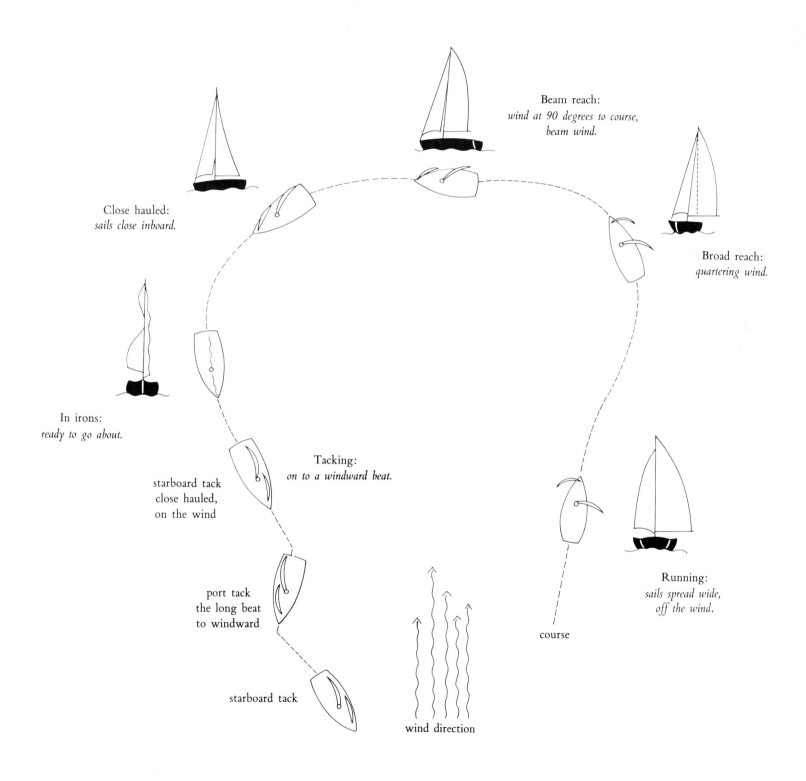

Beam reach:
wind at 90 degrees to course,
beam wind.

Close hauled:
sails close inboard.

Broad reach:
quartering wind.

In irons:
ready to go about.

Tacking:
on to a windward beat.

starboard tack
close hauled,
on the wind

Running:
sails spread wide,
off the wind.

port tack
the long beat
to windward

course

starboard tack

wind direction

The diagram gives a highly simplified outline of the positions of sail in relation to wind and course direction.

HMS *Endeavour*

THE GREAT SOUTH LAND REDISCOVERED

For thousands of years our vast island continent lay relatively undisturbed, only thinly populated by a people living within the limiting land. Isolated by sea, it was almost unknown to the outside world.

Then in the sixteenth century came the expansionist European adventurers. First there came the Spanish and Portuguese who voyaged our northern waters, then the Dutch who touched many points on our western coast, as well as Tasmania and New Zealand. Then came the French and British as rivals. Names on charts pay tribute to all these intrepid men. But this book must start with James Cook; although his story is well known, the full value of his work is not widely appreciated. His tale can be retold many times.

When he sailed on his first voyage in August 1768 only a few places on our west coast were known to the British and in the Pacific Ocean very little had been discovered or defined. After Cook's third voyage little of major significance in Oceania remained "incognita"—only filling in the details remained.

Officially his first voyage was to observe the transit of Venus which was recorded at Tahiti on 3 July 1769. He then set sail into the unknown South Pacific. In the process he discovered the Leeward Islands, Rurutu and other groups. He continued south-westwards to circumnavigate both islands of New Zealand, making an accurate survey of the coastline.

He then turned westwards and met the Australian coast at what is now known as Point Hicks (Victoria), named to honour one of his lieutenants. Next heading northwards along the coast, he anchored and planted the British flag at Botany Bay, so called because of the rich variety of flora collected most notably by Joseph Banks and recorded by Sidney Parkinson, the artist on the expedition. While these gentlemen were busy botanising a chart of the bay was completed, to be used by the First Fleet eighteen years later.

Cook then sailed north along the coast through the unchartered Great Barrier Reef. In July 1770 his ship was badly holed by a sharp coral reef. But with masterly seamanship the damage was fothered, that is covered with a canvas skin, and the stout ship was beached and repaired in what is now called Endeavour River. Repairs were completed by 6 August 1770 and Cook started the homeward journey, on the way planting the flag at Possession Island. The return voyage was via Torres Strait, Batavia (Jakarta) and the Cape of Good Hope to Plymouth where the *Endeavour* arrived in July 1771. Added to this great maritime accomplishment was a medical one—the successful introduction aboard ship of a new dietary routine which consisted mainly of sauerkraut and other pickled greens.

Endeavour is depicted here off the south-east corner of Australia pounding her way northwards through the lumpy seas that arise when the west wind blows. She is carrying working rig as described in William Falconer's Marine Dictionary *(1770), ". . . every advantage of sailing is retained by three masts and a bowsprit."*

HMS *ENDEAVOUR*

Some seamen died owing to causes such as dysentery and tropical diseases, but scurvy, the dread of a long sea voyage, took none of Cook's men.

For this epic voyage Cook chose the little barque *Earl of Pembroke*—a hard-working humble collier built at Whitby a short distance from his birthplace in Yorkshire. After extra cabins had been added and other alterations made to accommodate the scientists and artists, she was renamed *Endeavour*.

Her length was 105 ft (32 m), her breadth 29 ft (8.8 m) and her depth 20 ft (6.1 m). When she left England, crowded with a complement of seamen, officers, marines and scientific personnel—a total of ninety-four men—and fully provisioned for the long voyage, she drew over 13 ft (3.9 m) of water, leaving a freeboard of less than 6 ft (1.8 m)—not much for the unknown seas she was to encounter. Cook's choice was wise: her shape, bluff in the bow and round in the beam but flat-bottomed and of relatively small draught, qualified her for the task.

Cook's later explorations of the Pacific ranging south to the Antarctic and north to Arctic Alaska, used ships of a grander type. But although *Endeavour* was laid up, it was not the end of her story. Another exciting chapter followed.

In the late 1780s she was sold by the Admiralty to a French business company who fitted her out for whaling in the West Atlantic. She was renamed *La Liberté* and, under command of an American whaling captain, operated from Boston, Massachusetts.

Once again in the history of both nations Britain and France were at loggerheads and it was the unhappy duty of the Royal Navy to harass all shipping flying the French flag. *La Liberté* was one of the first victims of such naval action, when the British fired on her rigging. This tactic, well known in the days of sail, was used to disable rather than sink a vessel so that she could be "taken prize". Despite the generally inaccurate gunnery of the time, the British cannons found their mark. But no prize was taken for, with her sails in tatters but little damage to her stout timbers, *La Liberté* found refuge in Rhode Island Sound.

She was still whaling, according to an entry in Newport Harbour Masters' log, in 1794. After that records become vague but *Endeavour* did not fade into complete oblivion. Eventually she was broken up and her timbers were made into tables, walking sticks and other artefacts, which now stand as reminders of her in many American homes and museums. When Thomas Sopwith challenged for the America's Cup in 1934, the City of Newport, Rhode Island, presented him with a carved crown from the old ship's timbers. His yacht was called *Endeavour II*, still a proud name.

The First Fleet

FOUNDATION AND SETTLEMENT

26 January 1788 was a great day in Port Jackson. The log of Surgeon General John White recorded: "Weather clear, light S.S.E. breezes, temperature 70, barometer 29.98." This calm high afternoon scene was the sparkling backdrop as the fleet sailed through the heads of Port Jackson into the quiet waters of the harbour.

Surgeon White went on to describe Port Jackson as:

> *... the finest and most extensive harbour in the universe and at the same time the most secure being safe from all the winds that blow, it is divided up into a great number of coves to which his Excellency has given different names, that on which the town is to be built, is called Sydney Cove. It is one of the smallest in the harbour but the most convenient as ships of the greatest burden can with ease go into it and heave out close to the shore.*

It was the end of a weary voyage of over eight months. One thousand, three hundred and fifty souls crammed into eleven small ships brought seeds of a European culture to the shores of an old, enigmatic continent. Who among them at that tense time could have imagined the story of settlement and statehood that was to follow?

Sirius and *Supply*, the two naval vessels, formed the escort for a convoy of nine chartered merchant ships. Pride and favourite of the fleet was a little eight-gun brig, HMS *Supply*, a mere 70 ft (21 m) long and 26 ft (7.9 m) wide. On leaving Portsmouth she soon demonstrated her sailing qualities as tender to the fleet, mothering the much troubled stragglers, relaying signals and moving ahead of the flagship when necessary. It was her officers and crew who planted the flag claiming the new land for Britain and, when all other ships had departed and *Sirius* was wrecked, she alone of the First Fleet remained. For over twenty years she provided aid and protection to the settlement, bringing food from as far away as the Cape of Good Hope and the Dutch East Indies when starvation threatened. It is believed she ended her days on a Port Jackson beach, dismantled for her timbers.

The flagship, HMS *Sirius*, was a full-rigged ship, 110 ft (34 m) long and 32 ft (9.8 m) wide and armed with twenty guns. She had been built as a merchant ship for the British East India Company in 1770. The navy bought her for use as a store ship during the American war and she later served in the West Indies. Although her captain described her as "well-suited for the voyage", to other writers on board she seemed a sluggish and awkward ship. At one stage before her naval career she was almost burnt out. Nevertheless good seamanship ensured her success in her appointed task as flagship, although, sadly, this was her last long voyage. She was wrecked while serving the new settlement on Norfolk Island.

Of the convict transports, many logs, diaries and letters described the hardship of the voyage in intimate details. Every ship developed its own pesonality and although they are not all illustrated here they cannot be ignored.

The largest of the fleet was the barque-rigged *Alexander*, 114 ft (35 m) long and 31 ft (9.5 m) wide. She carried 195 male convicts, who gave a lot of trouble during the voyage; floggings were commonplace. On her return

HMS *SUPPLY* and HMS *SIRIUS*

voyage all but four of her crew died of scurvy and she continued the voyage with survivors of *Friendship*, which was scuttled, her crew being similarly decimated by scurvy. *Alexander* was still working in 1808.

Scarborough, barque-rigged, was 110 ft (34 m) long and 30 ft (9.2 m) wide. She carried 208 male convicts and had a good deal of disciplinary trouble, including a mutiny attempt in the first few weeks of the voyage. Punishments of 150 lashes were meted out to some of her marines and seamen. On the return voyage she took back to England a lucrative tea cargo from China. Her merchant owners enjoyed the profits of her charter, and she made the voyage again with the second fleet.

Prince of Wales, 103 ft (31 m) long and 29 ft (8.8 m) wide, carried forty-nine female convicts and one male convict. Crew members fought for female favours and floggings were common. On the return voyage her master and fourteen seamen succumbed to scurvy but she was able to pick up fresh crew members at Rio. Nevertheless it was a slow voyage home to England which took two years in all. Sometime after 1797 *Prince of Wales* changed registration, which she did several times, so that record of her eventual fate is lost.

Friendship was a brig somewhat larger than HMS *Supply* and, like her, a good sailer. However, with seventy-six male and twenty-one female convicts the brig acquired a reputation for trouble between the sexes. She struck serious misfortune on her return voyage; scurvy depleted her crew and she was scuttled in the Straits of Macassar, the surviving crew members joing *Alexander*. *Friendship* was the only convict transport of the First Fleet that failed to return to England.

Charlotte, 105 ft (32 m) long and 28 ft (8.5 m) wide, had a slow and sickly voyage, but with eighty-eight male and twenty female convicts there were some exciting moments. A child was born aboard and christened Charlotte; and while moored in Rio harbour some of the convicts passed to the crew counterfeit coins which they had ingeniously made while at sea. *Charlotte* sailed back to England with a cargo of China tea, after which she returned to merchant service in the Liverpool-Jamaica trade and later in Canadian service until lost off Newfoundland in 1818.

Lady Penrhyn, 103 ft (31 m) long and 27 ft (8.2 m) in the beam, carried 101 female convicts and a troublesome crew, some of whom were put aboard HMS *Sirius* for disciplinary treatment. Her rebellious women convicts were punished by being placed in iron fetters and having their heads shaved. Nevertheless this transport had an almost clean bill of health on arrival in Port Jackson, and like the other chartered East Indiamen she returned to England with a profitable cargo of China tea. Back in merchant service *Lady Penrhyn* had many changes of owner before apparently being lost at sea in the West Indies, although reports are difficult to confirm.

Fishburn was a store ship of 378 tons (384 t). Apart from a report of a seamen's strike over pay and conditions prior to sailing, little seems to have been recorded of her. It is known that she was built in Whitby and chartered from a Mr Leighton, but after her voyage with the First Fleet she faded out of the records.

This, then, is the setting at about 4 p.m. on that day in 1788. His Majesty's brig Supply *is at anchor close inshore, having arrived the previous day. Coming up astern is the flagship of the fleet, HMS* Sirius, *shaking the wind out of her foresails and holding the pressure in reduced main and mizzen as her helmsman brings her up. As all sails back, her way stops and the anchor is let go. By dusk all the fleet is in and secure.*

Golden Grove, a store ship of 375 tons (381 t), was also built in Whitby for Mr Leighton. With the chaplain of the colony, the Reverend Mr Johnson, and his wife as passengers, she had a relatively peaceful voyage, despite losing her fore-top gallant mast four times. After her return to England she worked on the Newcastle, Liverpool and West India runs.

Borrowdale, also a store ship of 375 tons (381 t), was built in Sunderland in 1785. She appears to have enjoyed an unsensational voyage, performed her duties of provisioning the colony without drama, and seems to have disappeared into the pages of history after her return to England.

The epic voyage of the First Fleet stretched over more than 24 000 kilometres. To catch the favourable winds the ships travelled twice across the Atlantic from Tenerife to Rio de Janeiro to Cape Town. They took on fresh fruit, meat and wine at every port available, and much livestock and grain necessary for the survival of the settlement to be was loaded at Cape Town. It was a triumph of organisational and navigational skills and also reflected credit on the chart work of Captain James Cook.

The loss of many lives was expected, but in fact only forty-nine deaths occurred and many of the victims were mortally ill before the voyage commenced, owing largely to the malnutrition and brutality of English gaols. All through the wearying voyage, the insistence on cleanliness, as much exercise as cramped conditions allowed, and the rigorous discipline of shipboard life brought benefits to many of the convicts. Later transportation fleets were neither as well organised nor as well governed by such enlightened and humane principles, evidence of which was the heavy loss of life aboard these subsequent voyages—deaths numbering in the hundreds were a common statistic.

Mr King's diary for 26 January 1788 concludes:

Afternoon, the Union Jack was hoisted and the Marines being drawn up under it, the Governor and officers to the right and the convicts to the left, their Majesties' and the Prince of Wales' health, with success to the Colony, was drunk in 4 glasses of porter, after which a feu-de-joie was fired and the whole gave three cheers.

Tom Thumb

EXPLORATION BEGINS

The sight of "boating people", or Sunday sailors, crowded into an eight-foot dinghy is commonplace in our harbours nowadays; it is sometimes comic, but with clumsy seamanship it can be precarious even in calm waters. The thought of a similar-sized boat crewed by two men and a boy making a long voyage in a seething, rolling open sea seems almost incredible. But 200 years ago seamen were of a different species of mankind—they must have been—and different too were their ships.

After settlement at Sydney Cove the need to know the environment became urgent. Investigations probed inland and seawards; it was the sea that provided our contours and beside the sea our capital cities grew. Cook had marked the coastline well and examined Botany Bay and a few other features in detail, but little was known of many other river mouths, bays and harbours on our long coastline. Later explorers had the task of mapping these.

The most famous of these maritime explorers were George Bass and Matthew Flinders. Bass was naval surgeon and Flinders a master's mate; both were Lincolnshire men. They met while serving in HMS *Reliance*, and with common interests became firm friends. Flinders in his *Voyage to Terra Australis* wrote:

> *In George Bass I had the happiness to find a man whose ardour for discovery was not to be repressed by any obstacle, nor deterred by any danger and with this friend a determination was formed of completing the examination of the East Coast of New South Wales by all such opportunities as the duty of the ship and procurable means would admit.*

Tom Thumb, a small rowing boat "8 ft. on the keel" was that "procurable means". That keel length may have permitted several centimetres more of overall length, about the same as the average modern dinghy, but her timber construction would have been stouter and her lines fuller and with more freeboard than today's craft. Rigged with the simplest of sail design, the spritsail, the most popular arrangement for small craft as pictured in the famous English and Dutch paintings of the time, it needed only two spars, one for the mast and one for the peak of the sail, three stays to hold the mast up and one sheet to trim the sail.

To sail the little craft in the Pacific coastal swells, one man handled the sheet, easing or hauling as the sea and wind demanded, the other had the steering oar, the sweep, to keep a steady heading and the boy bailed for dear life to prevent filling. Tight teamwork and concentration were essential: the slightest error in responding to the sea's action would have been fatal.

Bass, Flinders and the boy, William Martin, set out from Port Jackson in October 1795. They sailed southwards into Botany Bay and rowed up the Georges River for about 32 kilometres. The voyage lasted nine days and the favourable report to Governor Hunter resulted in the establishment of a depot named Bankstown.

They returned to the duties of the ship back on board HMS *Reliance*, but not for long. It would almost seem that exploration was a form of leisure hours relaxation. Within a few months all three were off again, in a slightly larger *Tom Thumb*, on a second voyage which provided many perils and discoveries. It was no sailing picnic.

It was in March 1796 when they set out to examine the coast south of Botany Bay. A southerly current and a northerly wind pushed them beyond the present site of Bulli and they ran for shelter under a headland named by Cook-Red Point. Thoroughly soaked and waterlogged, *Tom Thumb II* was beached and while stores were drying out Flinders went in search of fresh water. The aid of some Aborigines led them to a small rivulet, and here Lake Illawarra was sighted. It was first named Tom Thumb's Lagoon on Flinders' chart.

The return voyage was even more hazardous—Flinders' journal contains the simple, but dramatic statement, "The shade of the cliffs over our heads and the noise of the surf breaking at the foot were the direction by which our course was steered parallel to the coast." Heavy weather persisted and at Wattamolla, now part of Sydney's Royal National Park, mast and sail were shipped and again shelter was taken. After a short rest they headed northwards for about 6 kilometres to enter Port Hacking, one of the original objectives of the expedition. On 2 April they sailed sedately to mooring back in Port Jackson alongside HMS *Reliance* and back again to shipboard duties.

On 3 December 1797 Bass went south again, this time in a 28 foot (8.5 m) whaleboat manned by six naval oarsmen but without Flinders who was otherwise occupied. Turning west at Cape Howe, the south-east corner of Australia, he reached Western Port Bay, marking many points and harbours on the voyage. At Wilson's Promontory he met a party of escaped convicts, taking two aboard and provisioning the others to assist them to return to Sydney.

This voyage lasted from early December to 24 February, in the same season and on the same sea that have forced many much larger and better equipped boats of the Sydney–Hobart yacht race to seek shelter or withdraw from the event. To quote Flinders once again: "A voyage expressly undertaken for discovery, in an open boat, in which 600 miles [960 km] of coast [were explored], mostly in a boisterous climate has not perhaps its equal in the annals of maritime history."

George Bass and Matthew Flinders came together again on another voyage of exploration which was to be their last together. This was on the 20 ton cutter *Norfolk* on 7 October 1798. This voyage lasted almost three months during which Van Diemen's Land was circumnavigated, and many features were recorded and charted. The stormy stretch of sea separating the island state from the mainland was named in honour of Bass. George Bass was invalided out of the navy and died on the way home to England. Matthew Flinders continued his career and added another stirring chapter to the story of Australia's maritime exploration.

Tom Thumb is shown as she works southward down the coast in a following sea with the wind over her stern quarter. In this situation, any slip of concentration or failure of coordination between helmsman and sheet hand working the sail and Tom Thumb would have "broached to", that is, turned into the wave trough and rolled over. The painting illustrates the skilful seamanship of those men.

TOM THUMB

Investigator

THE COASTLINE CHARTED

In the late 1790s many small boats ventured out along the coastline to the north and south of Port Jackson, some with exploratory intent, others in pursuit of convicts. It was on one of the latter excursions that coal was first discovered, which led to the establishment of a coastal mining settlement in the south and later of Newcastle. It was another voyage of discovery that took Matthew Flinders north in a 25 ton sloop to Moreton Bay and Hervey Bay in the north after his companion in exploration, George Bass, had sailed off home to retirement. However, in 1800, after six years in the colony, Flinders returned to London and to the direct command of the Lords of the Admiralty.

It was they who commissioned his most memorable quest—the circumnavigation of "Terra Australis". Fired by the knowledge that the French were preparing an expedition for the same purpose, the Admiralty acted quickly. In January 1801 Flinders was put in command of HMS *Investigator*. He described her as "a North Country built ship of 334 tons [339 t] and in form nearly resembled the description of vessels recommended by Captain Cook as best calculated for voyages of discovery". She was in fact the collier *Xenophon* purchased by the navy, of about the same dimensions as the old *Endeavour*. The best of many books about this voyage is Flinders' own account and all the following quotations are from this source.

The meticulous Flinders took charge of refitting her for the voyage. A spare rudder was put on board and long guns were replaced by light carronades to gain space for extra water tanks, extra ventilation to cabins, and extra accommodation for the scientists and the artists. In addition to the usual rations there were mirrors, combs, knives, beads, earrings and linen "to trade with the natives". With thought to the health of his crew he also included extra quantities of vinegar, lime juice, and sauerkraut, the first as a mild disinfectant, the latter to prevent scurvy. The directors of the East India Company donated £1200 "table money", an early form of sponsorship.

After some delay *Investigator* eventually slipped her moorings at Spithead and set sail on 18 July 1801. She was a happy, healthy ship. Three months out and bound for Cape Town, Flinders wrote:

> I had begun very early to put into execution the beneficial plan first practised and made known by the great Captain Cook. It was standing orders that every fine day the decks and cockpit should be cleaned, washed and aired with stoves and sprinkled with vinegar, care was taken to prevent people sleeping on decks and lying down in wet clothes and once a fortnight or three weeks their beds and contents of their chests and bags were opened out and exposed to the sun and air.

⚓ *The painting depicts* Investigator *coming to anchor in Port Phillip Bay towards dusk on 26 April 1802. She grounded twice on shallows. The empty davits, projecting from the poopdeck, indicate that a boat and crew went ahead to sound a channel. Her jib is eased off and sails on the foremast are shaking, ready to be "backed" to stop or "filled" to maintain steerage way. This is the view the boat's crew would have seen.*

HMS *INVESTIGATOR*

Discipline on the ship, from what is recorded in Flinders' narrative, seems to have been fairly relaxed. Apart from simple cases such as drunkenness (quite common in these conditions), there is little record of any of the sort of treatment made notorious by stories of Captain Bligh, with whom Flinders had served as a youth. Furthermore, "on Sunday and Thursday the company mustered, every man clean shaven and dressed and when evenings were fine drum and fife announced the forecastle be the scene of dancing, nor did I discourage any other playful amusements which might be more to the tastes of sailors." Flinders was happy with the condition of his "people" and hoped to shorten his stay in Cape Town to leave more time to spend the summer working on the long unknown coast of Terra Australis. He was not so happy about the condition of his ship: before they had reached Cape Town a leak developed and eighteen days were lost in repairs. The next leg was a quiet thirty-two day crossing of the Indian Ocean.

Investigator made landfall in Western Australia, then known as "New Holland"—the Dutch had been there before and there was a belief that Terra Australis was divided by sea running north and south, New South Wales being the eastern land mass. Cape Leeuwin and Nuyts Point, first sighted by the Dutch in 1627, were passed and in the evening of 8 December King George Sound, where Albany now stands, was entered and surveyed.

From here on 3200 kilometres of heat-hazed coastline stretched enigmatically eastwards and it was here that Flinders' most significant discoveries were made. In search of a sea link to the Gulf of Carpentaria, he kept close inshore, the sight of breaking surf being his guide. Often he sent a boat ashore for closer investigation, and on one such venture a boat and crew of eight were lost in the steep surf. The curving coast of the Great Australian Bight was turning south and some disappointment was felt as no opening to the north appeared, but then a change in the currents and sea patterns induced Flinders to alter course northwards. He found his way into Spencer Gulf and St Vincent Gulf, but these were both found to be landlocked at the northern end. Carefully charting them, he named many points after townships in his native county: Port Lincoln, Dennington, Boston Bay and others. Kangaroo Island was visited, and in these waters he met and dined with the Frenchman Nicolas Baudin on *Le Géographe*, in April 1802. After a mutually interesting conference they parted company after two days, on 9 April. The meeting gave Encounter Bay its name.

Flinders continued his easterly course towards Bass Strait, tacked across to King Island, then returned to the rugged Victorian coastline in search of Bass's Western Port Bay. Approaching this, he sighted a rocky point which forms the easterly end of the entrance to Port Phillip Bay. His own words best describe the event:

> . . . *on the west side of the rocky point there was a small opening with breaking water across it, however, on advancing a little more westward the opening assumed a more interesting aspect and I bore away to have a nearer view. A large extent of water presently became visible within side, although the entrance seemed to be very narrow and there was in it strong ripplings like breakers. I was induced to steer in at half past one, the ship being close upon the wind and every man ready for tacking at a moment's warning.*

It was thought this was Western Port Bay, although it did not correspond with Bass's description. Twice *Investigator* grounded inside the bay, and Flinders sent out a boat to sound for a channel ahead. The painting shows her sails shaking as anchors are prepared to be dropped near where the popular township of Sorrento now stands. Six days were spent in a thorough examination of the bay, after which, as supplies were now becoming short, Flinders set sail for Sydney. The Heads were sighted on 8 May and in the following afternoon *Investigator* dropped anchor in the calm waters of Sydney Cove.

The first half of the voyage had been eminently successful: the southern coastline had been amply charted. In this spirit of success and despite the comforts of Sydney, Flinders itched to get on with the job. No weather bureau forecasts were available in those days and he was anxious to be off and in the tropics before the monsoon season.

It was planned that *Lady Nelson* would assist *Investigator*, especially for inshore and river work, and the two ships left Sydney on 22 July heading northwards. It soon became obvious, however, that the little brig was too slow, and indeed a hindrance, and when her main sliding keel was damaged on a shoal she returned to Sydney.

Flinders pressed on alone through the labyrinth of reefs. He passed Cape York, sailing into Torres Strait, which the Portuguese had previously visited, then south into the Gulf of Carpentaria where excellent chart work was done. Next he headed round the "top end", marking Melville Bay, Wessel Islands, Arnhem Land, the last in honour of the Dutch, and many other points, then on to Timor.

It was in these tropic seas that more serious trouble set in. Damp, sleepless nights and hot steamy sudden storms impaired the health of his "people". They had had only one fresh meat meal—on the King's Birthday—and vegetables had been in short supply in Sydney. Debilitating dysentery, which had started in the Gulf of Carpentaria, had now spread through the ship, and soon scurvy also took its toll. Tropical waters accelerated the deterioration of *Investigator*'s already damaged timbers and Flinders was faced with a race against death. Setting course southwards and then eastwards across the Bight, he "carried all possible sail day and night" and reached Sydney in June 1803.

The outline of Australia had been surveyed so effectively that most of Flinders' chart can still be used today. A thousand or more plant species had been added to the scientists' collection and some excellent drawings by artist William Westall are cherished in our national collections. The circumnavigation was a great achievement, but it had cost greatly in life and suffering.

After a thorough examination *Investigator* was condemned as totally unfit for further exploration. Flinders' final log entry expresses the melancholy duty of paying off:

1803 Friday 22 July, At moorings in Sydney Cove. Light airs and fine weather, people empld shifting chests on board Porpoise. *Discharged from the service, 9 petty officers and men, on board* Bridgewater *for a passage, the surgeon to sick quarters, one midshipman and on to the* Porpoise *for passage to England, the Commander and remaining officers and people, the naturalist, astronomer and painter of natural history remained behind in New South Wales until a new* Investigator *may come to complete the voyage. At sunset, hauled down the pennant.*

Flinders joined *Porpoise* for the voyage home but the ship was wrecked in what is now marked as Wreck Reef, about 320 kilometres east of Rockhampton. He returned to Sydney in a ship's boat and resumed his voyage in command of the 29 ton schooner *Cumberland*.

More misfortune befell Matthew Flinders. He was imprisoned by the French at Mauritius, where he called for provisions on his way home. War had broken out again between Britain and France. Napoleon's seapower was crushed at Trafalgar in 1805 but it was not until October 1810 that a sickened Flinders stood on his native shore. It was on his deathbed that he received the first proofs of his magnificent work, *A Voyage to Terra Australis*.

Ironically, *Investigator* was patched up in Sydney and sailed back to England in 1805. Of her later fate little is known although, according to a contemporary journal, *Mariner's Mirror*, *Investigator* was sold by the navy into Merchant Service, ending her days as a hulk in Port Phillip and broken up in 1872.

HMS *Lady Nelson*

THE GOVERNOR'S MESSENGER

As the general shape of Australia started to become clear, the initial accidental marking of the coastline in spots by seamen blown off course was replaced by the more deliberate work of Cook and Flinders. While defence was the major intent of official exploration, it was the scientific discoveries they made that captured the public imagination and ships began to be commissioned which catered for the widest aims of exploration. The early navigators made do with ships of varying types simply fitted out for the specific purpose. Carracks were used by Spain and Portugal; the Dutch used galliots and flutes. Cook's *Endeavour* was a collier, Flinders' *Investigator* a cargo vessel of similar design, Baudin's *Le Géographe* a corvette. As yet no class of vessel had developed specifically for exploration.

Rivalry from France was keen, and the need for a ship specially built for exploration soon became evident to Admiralty in London. Accurate, detailed chartmaking required the ability to work in shallow inshore waters, as well as to make long passages. For this purpose the brave little brig HMS *Lady Nelson* was built.

She was designed by Captain Schanck, whose name is commemorated by a cape on Victoria's coast. Launched at Deptford on the Thames in 1799, she was rated at 60 tons (61 t), measured a mere 52 ft (16 m) long and about 15 ft (4.6 m) wide, and had the shallow draught essential for her assignment. As the diagram shows, she was fitted with three "sliding keels", or centre boards, as today's trailer sailors would know them.

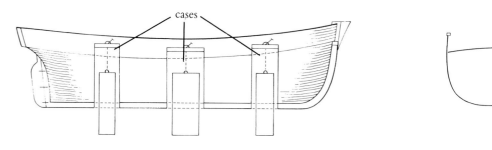

The sliding keels (centre boards) in HMS Lady Nelson.

With boards up she could operate in 6 ft (1.8 m) of water. To sail "on a wind" (i.e. with the wind coming from forward) the forward board would be down; "on a reach" (i.e. wind abeam, the wind coming from the side) the midship board, or all three at the discretion of the master, would be down; "running" or "off the wind" (i.e.

Here Lady Nelson *is shown with all sails set on a "quartering breeze", rolling slightly. As Lieutenant Grant describes it in his journal, "owing to her flat bottom she rose like a cork on the top of every wave."*

HMS *LADY NELSON*

Dutch galliot—de Vlamingh's Wezetje.
Sixteenth to seventeenth centuries.

Portuguese carrack.
Sixteenth century.

Dutch flute.
Seventeenth century.

French corvette—Baudin's Le Géographe.
Eighteenth century.

with the wind following) the after board would be down, holding her head away from the wind and preventing the dread of sailing men, the "broach to" (i.e. being caught side-on in a wave trough and rolled over).

The boards were lowered through a casing which reached to deck level, and any sea rising through this casing ran over the deck through the scuppers back into the sea. A simple sail plan also played an important part in her sailing qualities. The innovation was greeted with some hostility by the seamen of the day; they knew the sea, and many even doubted that her destination would be reached. Nevertheless, with a crew of fifteen under the command of Lieutenant Grant, her voyage to Port Jackson, via South America and South Africa, with a long break in Cape Town, took seven months—about average for those times.

It was planned that she would accompany and assist Flinders in his circumnavigation of Australia, but because of *Investigator*'s long delay at Spithead—a bureaucratic hold up—*Lady Nelson* sailed first in early 1800. She sailed to Sydney eastwards through Bass Strait, the first ship ever to do so. Under orders from Governor King she returned to the strait for a more detailed survey, marking King Island and other features. After further investigations of Western Port Bay, on 1 February 1801 she entered Port Phillip Bay, where Melbourne now stands, the first ship to sail through the notorious Rip.

In Sydney under a new commander she joined *Investigator* on her voyage northwards. Here the problems anticipated by the Thameside critics manifested themselves. She proved too slow to keep up with the larger and more robust *Investigator*, and her experimental boards proved difficult to handle by seamen inexperienced in this different style of sailing, so Flinders in his anxiety to proceed with his task sent her back to Sydney.

While general commercial trading in those days was the monopoly of the British East India Company, ship building and other maritime activities in the new colony were under the strict control of the Governor. *Lady Nelson* served him well. Her many missions included searches for escaped convicts, visits to the notorious Port Arthur convict settlement in Van Diemen's Land, now known as Tasmania, and help in the establishment of Risdon on Tasmania's Derwent River, under the command of Lieutenant Bowen. Governor King kept her busy with despatch work to the convict settlement on Norfolk Island, fetching grain from the Hawkesbury River settlements and coal from Newcastle, carrying building materials, troops and supplies to new settlements in Tasmania and New Zealand, and taking troops and settlers to the far north of Australia. She sailed via the Torres Strait and Timor islands to the then Dutch East Indies for food supplies in the hard times and enjoyed a richly varied career, vital to Australia's growth.

The little brig served the infant colony for twenty-five years under different commanders. Her useful career ended on Baba Island in Torres Strait when she was attacked by pirates and run ashore.

Brig *Union* & Schooner *Independence*

SEALSKINS AND WHALE OIL – THE FIRST EXPORTS

It was fifteen years after the first settlement in Sydney that the Governor authorised exploration to the south. Bass and Flinders opened the passage through the Bass Strait and soon this island-studded stretch of stormy seas was added to the charts. It was from these seas and islands that Australia's first export industry grew.

The abundance of whales in the southern seas of Australia had been noted earlier by convict ship captains and some of them, after discharging their sad human cargo, refitted their vessels for whaling, hoping to profit on the return voyage. Seals and whales provided the first valuable cargo from the new colony. Before long, men of many nationalities joined in the search.

The sealers kept close on the tracks of the chartmakers, very often going ahead to find anchorages and build shore bases which were not marked on the official charts until many years later. American River on Kangaroo Island, South Australia, was one of these.

Here, Matthew Flinders in HMS *Investigator* was working off the coast and met Frenchman Nicolas Baudin in the corvette *Le Géographe*. This was in 1802, only three years before the battle of Trafalgar, but despite the political tensions of the time, Flinders passed on knowledge from the discoveries he had made to his French counterpart. These were gentlemen of the sea.

Later, Baudin, while proceeding to chart the island in more detail, met up with an American sealing party under Captain Pendleton in his 120 ton (122 t) "snow", *Union*. At dinner with Baudin, Pendleton explained his purpose, a search for seal skins and oil for the rich markets of China. Baudin responded with all the courtesies of the seaman's code. He freely gave advice about fresh water, suitable anchorages and copies of Flinders' charts. Each mariner then continued on his own way. Pendleton soon found a snug anchorage and, leaving a small party ashore to build a "small schooner", his sealing party went on to collect a profitable cargo of over 5000 seal skins.

The *Sydney Gazette* of 8 January 1804 reported:

> On Friday arrived the ship Union, Captain Pendleton, from New York but last from Bass's Strait, whither she went to freight in skins and oil and has procured 5/6,000 of the former. She left New York in October 1802 and

Independence is shown being built on the beach, her foremast being stepped in an almost completed hull, while Union *sits quietly at anchor drying her sails in the warm still air. American River is now a popular holiday resort, and today this delightful area is dotted with yachts and other pleasure craft.*

Brig *UNION* and Schooner *INDEPENDENCE*

this port on 10th of October last and wintered at Kangaroo Island, where she stayed for upwards of 4 months, during which interval Captain Pendleton set out to build a small vessel of 30 tons burthen, named the Independence *now at Kangaroo Island whither he intends shortly to sail, having touched this port only to refresh.*

Union made a "grocery" run to Norfolk Island for Governor King and then returned to Kangaroo Island in April 1804. Pendleton put sixteen of his original crew of thirty-eight aboard *Independence* and together the two ships sailed for Sydney with 12 000 skins. Later, while engaged in the sandalwood trade with Fiji, she got trapped among the reefs and was lost with all hands. *Independence* continued her sealing activities, but after leaving Sydney in June 1805 she disappeared in the vast expanse of the Southern Pacific Ocean.

It is hard to get exact statistics of those free and wild days, especially of non-government-controlled shipping. It is known that there was a sizeable, well-settled population already on the island long before the South Australian Company was founded in 1836.

A Sydney report in *The Australian* of 9 March 1826 states:

Kangaroo Island, situate just through the Straits, it would seem has got quite a population of its own and we suppose is in a condition to select a king and enact laws, it is said that there are at present upwards of 200 souls vegetating at this convenient spot. 30 men and 40 black women independent of numerous progeny contrive to make themselves quite comfortable in their snug retreat.

There is evidence to indicate the spot where *Independence* was built and to suggest that the local cypress pine, *Callitris propinqua*, was cut for her timbers. Her tonnage is given variously, ranging from 30 to 40 tons, but it is known that she was a small topsail schooner, the first ship to be built in South Australia.

Union was a snow, a fashionable rig in the 1800s. Like the brig of the day it was two masted and square rigged on both but it had a supplementary mast behind the main, carrying a try sail, or gaff spanker. Her 120 tons burthen would indicate the space of a modest three bedroom house. In ships like these a crew of fifteen to twenty-five men would live and work for periods of two years or more.

Colonial Brig *Amity*

WESTERN AUSTRALIA CLAIMED

It is often the case that the quiet little fellow does most of the less glamorous work but is soon forgotten, and it is often that least honour goes to the most deserving. Many small ships—brigs, cutters, schooners and ketches—that were engaged along the newly marked coastline in whaling, sealing and trading are now hardly remembered. It is to the credit of the proud citizens of the City of Albany that the brig *Amity* is not one of these. They have built a new *Amity* and sat her on the city's foreshore. Except for her canvas and related rigging she is as close to a faithful replica as could be achieved.

The brig rig—two masts, square-rigged—was the most utilitarian of the day. It was economical to build and to operate—a smaller crew was needed—and this rig therefore offered a better business proposition for the smaller enterprising merchant. Such a ship was of course much less comfortable than the large three-masters, but comfort was not an important commodity, nor it seems was life itself in those early days of Australia's history.

Britain's famous oak forests were by the 1800s almost denuded for the building of ships for the Royal Navy and, mainly because of lack of suitable timbers, *Amity* was built in Canada in 1816 of black birch, hackmatac and larch. She was 75 ft 6 ins (23 m) long, 21 ft 5 ins (6.5 m) wide and 11 ft 5 ins (3.5 m) deep in the hold. Headroom below decks averaged less than 5 ft (1.5 m). She was registered as 142 tons (144 t). These dimensions, though considered substantial at the time, are not much more than those of the modern "Maxi" yacht.

According to the laid-down practice of the times she was carvel built, i.e. with planks laid edge on edge. Her main mast would have reached 85 ft (26 m) above the deck; the foremast would have been slightly shorter. These two carried the square sails. Fore and aft sails, the jibs, were carried on forestays to the bowsprit and jib-boom, which also held up the mast, and a spanker was set abaft the main mast on a gaff and boom. These helped to balance the steering system.

Amity's working career commenced after the Napoleonic wars and the war of 1812 with America. In the piping days of peace she traded profitably across the Atlantic, carrying timbers from the New World to the Clydesdale shipyards and returning back loaded with Britain's industrial products, agricultural implements etc., and also carrying Scotland's most popular produce to warm the cockles of Canadian hearts.

A change in ownership in 1822 resulted in a new port of registry, Greenock, Scotland, and after some time trading to Ireland and along the coast she changed owners again. This time she went to a Scottish farming family, the Ralstons, who bought her for a passenger ship for migrants to New Holland and New South Wales. She set sail in 1823, taking the now established route to South America for fresh water and supplies, then heading south to the "roaring forties". She reached Hobart Town on 16 April 1823, after a six-month voyage with passengers and cargo, according to the *Hobart Town Gazette*. She was next reported in the *Sydney Gazette* as "Landed 2 bulls and 4 cows from Scotland". Many of Australia's great cattle herds grew from farmer and shipowner Ralston's first shipment.

Colonial Brig *AMITY*

Amity traded along the coasts for a time and then was sold in Sydney to Governor Brisbane in 1824. The first voyage on official business took her to Hobart Town to the convict settlement of Van Diemen's Land with a cargo that included leg irons, handcuffs and convict clothing.

She was a busy little brig, making many useful trips to Hobart Town and Bass Strait and also playing a valuable part in the settlements on Moreton Bay and the Brisbane River.

But her voyage of greatest consequence was westward. In the 1820s there was a strong fear that, while New South Wales had been claimed by the British, the land to the west, New Holland as it was still known, was open to settlement by other expansionist European powers, especially the French. Even though Waterloo and Trafalgar were well past, the old mutual mistrust persisted between the two powers, and the British realised it was no longer sufficient to simply plant the flag—settlement had to be established. This was *Amity*'s job which, when accomplished, secured forever Australia as the only continent of single nationhood.

Amity sailed from Port Jackson in November 1826 with Major Edmund Lockyer in command. The ship was carrying a captain, a sergeant, eighteen rank and file marines, twenty-three convicts, a surgeon, and Lieutenant Colson RN and his crew and other staff, together with supplies to last six months, and livestock and seeds for planting— quite a crowd to be accommodated in a vessel with one tween deck providing less than 5 ft (1.5 m) headroom. People over 5 ft tall had to find their way to the hammocks by a hands and knees manoeuvre.

Amity's voyage was a "long beat" of six weeks in weather modestly described by Lockyer as "boisterous"—it took three weeks to reach Hobart Town on the way westwards. On Christmas Day he sailed into King George Sound, his simple statement, "being late, did not land this evening but proposed to go ashore in the morning", giving no feeling of the historic significance of his voyage. He spent 100 days establishing the settlement now known as Albany and then returned to Sydney.

Within two years of this event, further exploration, directed from Sydney by Governor Darling, reached around to the long west coast, which had already been noted by Dutch, French and British navigators as early as 1696. Captain James Stirling in HMS *Success* explored further and fixed the sites of Fremantle and Perth.

Amity continued working in many capacities, whaling, sealing and trading on the Hobart register. In 1845, after more trips from Hobart, labouring in heavy winds, she struck a spit of sand near Flinders Island in Bass Strait. The strong wind and heavy sea drove her further ashore, where she was wrecked. Her owner, a Hobart butcher and her captain, mate and crew of eight men all got ashore. They were rescued by sealers, who gave them refuge until they found their way back to their homes in Tasmania.

The painting shows Amity *"on a fresh wind abaft the beam" with topgallants and royals furled, jibs and spanker set to ease the helm. Black and yellow was the fashionable livery of the merchant ship at this time.*

THE HENTY FAMILY SETTLE WEST VICTORIA

While the coastal trade was resulting in all the exciting growth radiating from Sydney, southern waters became a source of production of Australia's first export industry. Sealers and whalers had been busy in Bass Strait for many years. Hobart on the Derwent River and Launceston on the Tamar River were firmly established and Tasmania became the next centre of Australia's growth. It was from Tasmania that the Hentys and later John Batman crossed the strait to found what is now the state of Victoria. The Hentys made their memorable trip in their little ship *Thistle*.

Prior to this historic crossing *Thistle* had had a long and distinguished career with the British East India Company and had made many exciting voyages. Built in Calcutta in 1750, she made a trading voyage to Fremantle, Western Australia, in 1830 and another in the following year. The second voyage took her on through Bass Strait to Sydney thence northwards to the Timor Sea. On this trip her West Australian agent was on board but died during the voyage, and on her return to Fremantle *Thistle* was put up for sale. James Henty bought her for £650. In November of that year, with Stephen and John Henty on board, she sailed for Launceston, Tasmania, and was registered as a trading vessel serving mainly between Hobart and Sydney.

In 1833, whilst returning from another Western Australian voyage, *Thistle* called in for a cargo of whale oil at Portland Bay, where John Dutton had established a whaling settlement. It was here that Edward Henty found what he had been seeking for some time, good grazing land. The next voyage to the west was purely and simply an exploratory exercise. *Thistle* sailed up St Vincent Gulf, calling at Kangaroo Island, and along the South Australian coastline, then made a long beat across a stormy Great Australian Bight to Fremantle.

In April 1834 she was back in Launceston and in May she set off on another exciting voyage. This time it was to New Zealand to the rescue of the ship *John Dunscombe*, which had been reported captured by Maoris. *Thistle*'s captain was instructed by the owners to proceed to the rescue "of so many unfortunate people from the hands of savages", and to forego all profitable trading if necessary. However, after a hard journey across the Tasman in which she battled heavy seas that smashed her bowsprit and part of her bulwarks, all *Thistle* returned with to Tasmania was a cargo of flax, pork and timber.

Thistle, *sometimes described as a schooner of 60 tons (61 t) displacement, is listed as a brigantine in the* Launceston Advertiser *of May 1834. This would most likely have been her rig when she was in service with the East India Company and it is in this rig she is here illustrated battling a squall under reefed canvas and her topsail "coming in". She was eighty-seven years afloat and some of her stout "Sal" timbers* (Shorea robusta) *may still be seen at Port Fairy.*

Topsail Schooner *THISTLE*

Then came the historic voyage. The Henty family story is well chronicled, but their passage across Bass Strait is memorable for many reasons. It demonstrates the difficulties of sail and the temperament of the strait. On 13 October 1834, with Edward, son of Thomas Henty, on board and a cargo of seeds and agricultural implements, she sailed quietly from the Tamar River into a calm Bass Strait. On the second day out, she was within 8 kilometres of her destination, Portland Bay, when with gale force the wind changed and *Thistle* had to race back to shelter at King Island. Five times she started out and five times was forced back. On the sixth attempt after battling biting winds and big seas all the way she eventually made harbour. The trip had taken thirty-four days.

Henty's diary entry recording the event is brief on atmospherics but businesslike:

19 November 1834. Arrived in Portland Bay in the schooner Thistle—*cast anchor at 8 a.m. after a long and boisterous voyage of 34 days heavy weather. We lost 2 working bullocks, 2 cows, 2 calves and 12 heifers. Landed 13 heifers, 4 bullocks, 5 sows in pig, 2 turkeys, 2 guinea fowl, 6 dogs, seeds, plants, 1 whaleboat, 4 men, H. Camfield and myself, allowance of wages for 10/- per week and board. Fine day, wind S.E. light. Landed all cattle today by 1 a.m.*

For the following two years *Thistle* became the lifeline between Tasmania and the new pastoral settlement, and plied busily across the strait ferrying passengers, fruit trees, building material, seeds and cattle. On 7 November 1837 she sailed again to Portland and, after discharging her passengers and cargo she headed along the coast to Port Fairy to load a cargo of wattle bark. Here her luck ran out. For three days she had ridden quietly at anchor and becalmed, then a sudden strong south-westerly struck. Her anchor chain broke. A second anchor was dropped but also gave way, and *Thistle* grounded in the trough of a big wave. All hands got ashore safely but *Thistle* was lost—victim of another act of Bass Strait temper.

Cutter *Rebecca*

JOHN BATMAN BEGINS HIS "VILLAGE"

Henty's expedition excited the pioneering spirit of the colonists of Van Diemen's Land. Within a year of Henty's voyage, John Batman and Pascoe Fawkener joined in the search for new land across Bass Strait. There was some rivalry between these two gentlemen. The question of who actually was the founder of Melbourne is still in debate but John Batman's simple statement, "this is the place for a village", must be generally accepted. It is firmly embedded in the pavement of Flinders Street, Melbourne, it is supported by newspapers of the day, and it is commemorated by a plaque on the wall of a famous hotel.

The *Launceston Advertiser* of 21 May 1835 reported: "Mr. Batman with a number of attendants including Sydney natives left Georgetown this week in a small vessel commanded by Mr. Harwood for the purpose of exploring part of the same country." The *Hobart Town Courier* for 22 May 1835 reported:

> The Rebecca *sloop, the property of Mr. Robert Scott, sailed during the week for Port Phillip under charge of Captain J. B. Harwood, having on board several persons whose curiosity had led them to seek, in the uninhabited wilds of the coast of New Holland, a realisation of golden expectations. We doubt their success very much.*

It goes on, "Mr. Batman is aboard the *Rebecca* having under his charge several native blacks for the purpose of exploring the country."

Rebecca's charter cost Batman £12 10s per month. Archives contain much interesting and sometimes conflicting information, especially on the business aspect of the expedition, but of the "small vessel" herself, clear documentation is scarce.

The term sloop, particularly when used loosely by reporters of those days, described a variety of small vessels. *Rebecca* has also been described as a "cutter of 30 tons", a dimension which has only vague meaning in ship measurement systems today. It is known that she was built on the Tamar River in northern Tasmania by an English captain, Mr Plummer, who later helped develop Tasmania's apple-growing reputation. This meagre information, together with other factors such as "three attendants, crew", would suggest that she could have been typical of many small vessels that plied cargo on the British coastline at the time.

This could have been the scene about 10 a.m. on 29 May 1835. Batman's diary for that day reads:

> *This morning as soon as daylight appeared saw the heads of Port Philip about eight miles [13 km] off. With a fair wind we got between the heads about nine o'clock A.M., the tide running and nearly low water. A very heavy surf running at the entrance. The wind was light, and with some difficulty we got in; width about one mile and a quarter, the depth five and a half to seven fathoms of water. We got well into the port about ten o'clock, where the water is very smooth, and one of the finest basins of water I ever saw, and most extensive. I would not recommend any-one to come in until the tide was running in, when the surf is smooth at the mouth. As we were*

Cutter *REBECCA*

sailing up the port heard a dog on the shore howling. Cannot think what brought it there. Just called upon deck to see about 100 geese flying near the vessel; they seemed very large, and flew up the port before us. We anchored in a small bay about twelve miles up the port, and went on shore.

"Rebecca" appears to have been a popular name at that time: the shipping lists contain barques, ketches, brigs and other vessels of that name. What happened to Batman's "village" is well known—it is now the City of Melbourne—but this small vessel *Rebecca* seems to have disappeared into the haze of history.

Stoutly built, straight-stemmed and with beamy black-pitched hull, Rebecca is shown here at about 11.00 a.m. moving serenely and slowly with a fair light westerly wind on the quarter. She is rigged as a cutter with a long bowsprit and sliding top mast, loose-footed main, leg o'mutton top sail, a square sail set on the yard and headsails set on forestays.

SS Sophia Jane

THE FIRST STEAMBOAT AND STEAM SHIPPING COMPANY

The idea of using steam power to drive ships arose in Europe before 1800. In the early years of the new century it was applied to small craft working on the canals, rivers and lakes of Britain and America. Paddlewheels, a natural development from oars, made the most obvious means of propulsion. It was not long in the time scale of those days before an Australian decided to "give it a go". In March 1831 a little steamer was launched in Neutral Bay, Sydney, intended for the Parramatta service; but the first steamer to turn a paddle on Port Jackson was *Sophia Jane*.

The shipping column of the *Sydney Gazette* of 17 May 1831 announced her arrival: "From London, Pernambuco and the Cape, having left the former port on 16 December 1830, the steampacket *Sophia Jane*, Captain Biddulf, passengers, Mrs. Biddulf and family."

To the residents of Sydney the sea was a lifeline: a ship meant news from home. An arrival was always an event to relieve the feelings of isolation and folk would flock to the harbourside. Again quoting the *Sydney Gazette*: "Saturday last the inhabitants of Sydney had the extreme gratification of seeing for the first time a steam vessel floating, on the harbour." The report goes on, in the effusive journalese of the day,

> No expense has been spared for the comfortable accommodation of her passengers and her apartments are of the finest description. She has three separated cabins, one for gentlemen, one for ladies and another for steerage passengers. In the gentlemen's cabin 16 beds can be made up, in the ladies' 11 and in steerage 20 and in cases of emergency, extra beds can be prepared, making in all 54.

Sophia Jane was built in 1826 by Barnes and Miller, both of whom had previously worked with the pioneer of the steam engine, the famous James Watt. She is described as 126 ft (38.4 m) long on the deck, which must have included the forecastle and "fiddle" bow as well as the overhang of her counter stern, as the width of 20 ft (6.1 m) seems small in comparison. Paddle-boxes would have added at least 10 ft (3 m) more overall beam. Her 50 horsepower engines gave her a speed of 8 miles per hour (13 km per hour) "in calm water". Wood and coal stoked her furnaces.

Originally built for passenger traffic along Britain's coast and across to French ports, she was bought as a speculative venture by a group hoping to make a profit by selling her to the colonies. After arousing a good deal of interest but no buyers in Cape Town, she made Sydney her destination. The voyage was made under sail.

She was soon ready for service in Sydney and one of her first engagements was to tow the sailing ship *Lady Harwood* to the Heads. She presented a sight like Turner's painting "Fighting Temeraire" but with a happier mood.

⚓ *In the painting* Sophia Jane *is shown bowling along from Newcastle to Sydney under sail and steam with a fresh northerly behind her.*

SS SOPHIA JANE

All shipping saluted as she pulled the stately sailing ship down the harbour to set sail for London. The *Sydney Herald* of 12 June commented,

> *The ease and rapidity with which she towed the ship created the greatest admiration and applause. This is the first application of steam power to the purpose above mentioned that Australia can boast of and from the important benefit that must come to the colony by introduction of this valuable discovery we think that the proprietors of such vessels deserve every support that the government of the colony and the community at large can give them.*

It was good advertising. A few days later His Excellency the Governor, with a select party of the elite, breakfasted on board and enjoyed a harbour cruise to Parramatta. In the afternoon she steamed to Middle Harbour and out through the Heads, taking 35 minutes to return from the Heads to Fort Macquarie. The large party of prominent citizens on board were impressed and as a result, Australia's first steam shipping company was formed with all shares held by local business people and with *Sophia Jane* as their principal asset.

Sophia Jane's first trip under her new ownership was to the Hunter River. She left her wharf early in the morning, towed the ship *Emma* on the way out to the Heads and proceeded on to Newcastle, arriving there in mid-afternoon; she then went on to Green Hill (now called Morpeth) further along the river. Her return trip took 3 hours down river to Newcastle and 7 hours 40 minutes to her wharf in Sydney near Bathurst Street. Another account of *Sophia Jane*'s first voyage states she "departed Sydney at 7.13 a.m., arrived Newcastle at 3.13 p.m.". For the next twenty years she maintained a reliable service timetabled to the speed of her first coastal run. She called in at many ports along the New South Wales coast, and was the first steamer into Wollongong and other ports to the north and south of Sydney.

Her steam power allowed a regularity never possible to sailing ships. But the service *Sophia Jane* provided often took her into harbours for which she was not designed and involved frequent groundings on sandbars, so that after two decades her timbers had become badly strained. She was broken up in 1845 and her engines and boilers were fitted into a new steamer built in Sydney a year later.

Meanwhile, the little steamer *Surprise*, under construction in Neutral Bay when *Sophia Jane* made her great entry into Sydney, had served the Parramatta run very well; it can claim to be the forerunner of the modern Sydney Harbour ferry. The first ocean-going steamer built in Australia, *William the Fourth*, had also come into service to the northern ports. So competition in trade along the coast developed.

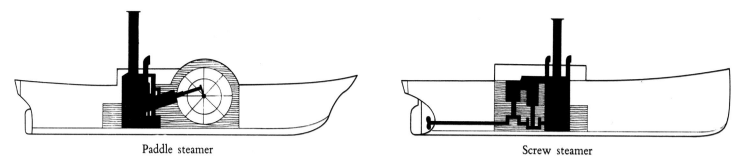

Paddle steamer   Screw steamer

Cut-away views of early paddle and screw steamers allow for a comparison of the ratio of engine and boiler space to hull space. The advantage in carrying space of the later mode of propulsion is clear.

PS *Experiment*

PADDLEWHEEL TRANSPORTS ON SYDNEY RIVERS

To the west of the growing city of Sydney were the fertile valleys of the Hawkesbury and Parramatta Rivers, which were the settlement's bread basket. Roads were poor, the load of the pack horse was limited and most of the wheat and other produce passed down these rivers to the hungry growing city. Barges, punts and wherries were the means of transport.

1832 saw the first paddle-driven ship built in Australia. Engineers, experts in the new invention of steam engines, and the capital to employ them were scarce in the fledgling colony, but resourcefulness and inventive ingenuity were plentiful and are now part of the pioneer legend. These qualities were certainly demonstrated by the aptly named ship *Experiment*, whose paddle power was provided by horse power—two live ones hitched to a treadmill which was linked to paddlewheels.

Her first trip, from Mr Wilson's wharf in Sydney to Parramatta, took six hours. Although this was reduced considerably as skills in operating the horses improved, the sight, smell and inefficiency of the equine treadmill proved unpopular with passengers. After two months' service she was advertised for sale, with the suggestion that the installation of a twelve horsepower steam engine would improve matters. This was done and together with another little steamer, *Australia*, she then maintained a regular service for five years with only two "days off".

With the rapid growth of Sydney, larger and faster ships took over the traffic and *Experiment* was sold to a Mr Pearce of Queensland for service between Brisbane and Ipswich; she went north in 1846.

The *Moreton Bay Courier* for 20 June 1846 welcomed her with an article headed "Local Intelligence":

The Experiment, *this steamer started from North Brisbane on her experimental trip to Ipswich on Wednesday morning last. Mr. Pearce, the owner and a select party on board were warmly greeted as they passed up the river by a large concourse of spectators who had assembled to witness her departure. Owing to the imperfect knowledge of the person acting as pilot, respecting the river flats, she got aground near the crossing place at Woogooroo and was detained until daylight the following morning, when she proceeded on her voyage and reached her destination at one o'clock. The Ipswich folk were delighted at her appearance among them and expressed their satisfaction by giving a hearty reception to Mr. Pearce and all those on board.*

It went on to state, "Mr. Pearce intends to accommodate parties of pleasure visiting the Bay." It described "the excellent accommodation consisting of a ladies' and gentlemen's cabin" and concluded: "on Tuesday Mr. Pearce applied to the magistrate for a licence for the sale of spirituous liquors on board, which was immediately granted."

She made occasional pleasure trips to Moreton Bay and carried many passengers on her 55 mile (88 km) trip between Brisbane and Ipswich, but general cargo was her main function—wheat, wool and other produce. Towing cargo-laden barges increased her capacity and costs were not high, but despite her value to local development the

PS *EXPERIMENT*

optimistic Mr Pearce soon learned that the hazards of operating a shipping business were as great as the hazards of the sea.

This notice in the *Moreton Bay Courier* tells the sad story:

Notice from the number of DEBTS due to the Experiment *steamer, the owner feels compelled to inform the public that no credit can be given in future and parties sending freight by her are requested to appoint an agent in Brisbane or Ipswich who will pay all accounts monthly, to prevent the detention of goods and consequent annoyance to the consignees, who are also requested to send instruction to their agents to mark all packages distinctly. All parties indebted are also required to pay up their accounts to the end of June, Ipswich 7 July 1847.*

Pearce ended his days as a clerk in a Brisbane gaol.

Experiment's dimensions are given as 80 ft (24 m) long, 12 ft 6 ins (3.8 m) wide and only 2 ft (0.6 m) draught. When she foundered at Brisbane in 1848, her engines were removed and installed in a newly built vessel, the *Hawk*, which continued the river and bay service for some years.

Experiment *is shown on the Bremmer River near Ipswich with a laden barge in the foreground. These barges increased her cargo capacity, and were left alongside a property to be loaded or unloaded by the farmer and were picked up on the return trip.*

PS *Rose*

THE HUNTER RIVER LINK

Sydney in 1800 was the heart of a vast land mass. But it was no faint heart. By 1830 its outward-reaching vitality extended to well-established settlements in Tasmania (Van Diemen's Land) and along the coast of New South Wales as far north as Moreton Bay and the Brisbane River. The only effective arteries linking these settlements were ships. These were sail-powered at first, but soon the advantage of steam power—the ease of navigation along narrow rivers to upriver settlements—outweighed the long-distance superiority of the wind-driven ships. By 1849 many steamers, built of timbers found in the area of service, were running fairly regular services. The first ocean-going steamer built in Australia was *William the Fourth*. She was timber built in 1831 on the Williams River, a tributary of the Hunter River, and provided a regular service to Newcastle and Maitland on those rivers for three years. When competition from new larger and faster steamers, like *Rose* and *Thistle*, became intense she was diverted to the Port Macquarie run and continued to provide a successful service to northern settlements for many years.

The growing demand from the settlements and the merchants was for more shipping. The *Sydney Morning Herald* of 31 July 1839 carried the following advertisement:

> *A meeting will be held at the Royal Hotel tomorrow 1 August to take into consideration a proposition for establishing a Steam Navigation company between Sydney and the Hunter River, with a view to obviating the great inconvenience and expense incurred from the present line of conveyance. It is requested that those gentlemen who feel interested in promoting this object will give their attendance.*

This resulted in the formation of the Hunter River Steamship Company, Australia's first. The company declined offers of any ship already in operation. They wanted the latest and ordered three iron-built steamers from England "of light draft and greatest obtainable speed": *Rose*, *Thistle* and *Shamrock*.

Rose and *Thistle* were sister ships, both built at Millwall on the Thames, with engines made in Manchester, giving a speed on trials of 12 statute miles (12 land miles per hour). Their dimensions were 150 ft (46 m) length, 20 ft (6.1 m) width plus the huge paddle-boxes of the time. They were of 275 tons (279 t) and drew 6 ft 6 ins (2 m). They had two masts and the rounded counter stern and clipper bow typical of the sailing ships of the time. *Shamrock*, Bristol built, was slightly larger and was rigged with three masts. All ships carried sail.

Rose was the first to arrive in Australia. She left London on 31 October 1840 for Sydney, but heavy weather in the Bay of Biscay forced her into Lisbon for repairs. From here she continued under sail to Cape Town, where she

Rose is shown in the picture approaching the cliffs of Kangaroo Point, as she heads down the Brisbane River to Moreton Bay and the open sea.

50

PS ROSE

William the Fourth

⚓ *On 21 February 1832, the* Sydney Gazette *recorded: "That beautiful specimen of colonial enterprise, the* William the Fourth, *made her maiden trip to the Hunter last week. She left Barker's Wharf at 7.30 in the evening, cleared the Heads in 44 minutes and made Newcastle at 6 o'clock the following morning."* William the Fourth *was the first ocean going steamer built in Australia and missed by only a few months being the first steamer to enter Sydney Harbour. Built of locally cut timbers at Clarence Town on the Williams River, her engine was installed by Mr Patterson, a millwright of the Phoenix Foundry, Sydney. She measured 80 ft (24 m) in length, 15 ft (5 m) at the beam, plus 5 ft (2 m) over the paddle boxes. She served the New South Wales coast for over thirty years and went to China in 1862.*

refuelled and completed her voyage under sail and steam. At Sydney Heads she was ordered on to Newcastle, arriving on 7 April 1841.

Rose maintained reliable service for passengers and varied cargoes between Sydney and Hunter River ports. The only reports of "incidents" seemed to concern the races with her rivals. Every ship had its patrons and betting was heavy. It was the "Colonials" versus the "Sterlings", Australian born versus British born. The *Herald* of 21 April 1841 reported:

Victoria *arrived in Sydney 10 minutes past 6 yesterday, then* Rose *afterwards, leaving Newcastle* Victoria *was two miles ahead and kept so for several miles, when a north easterly sprang up she set square sails, then* Rose *had none,* Victoria *gained 3 miles.* Rose *wanted slipping and it is expected she will make the passage in an hour less. If it does she must run fast. On 6 May* Rose *arrived ahead but* Victoria *had a heavy cargo and 19 horses on deck. 18 May was a dead heat. The average time from Newcastle to Sydney was eight hours.*

The Harbour Ferries

⚓ *In 1864 the Brighton and Manly Steam Ferry Company was formed, their first ship being the paddle steamer* Phantom, *built five years previously in Melbourne. She was 120 ft (37 m) long but only 13 ft (4 m) wide, and even with the width of her paddles added she must have provided an uncomfortable ride along the coast and across Sydney Heads. She was the first ship to wear the green hull and black-topped white funnel of the Manly Steamship Company and was sold out of the service in 1878.*

The racing rivalry provided excitement for the Sydneysiders and some motivation to the engineers. A slight increase in boiler pressure shortened the trip to 7½ hours. Then *Thistle* came onto the scene with a record of 6 hours 20 minutes. *Shamrock* became the favourite on the Sydney–Eden–Launceston run, as well as Sydney to Brisbane.

In October 1848 *Rose* extended her run to Brisbane, making what was then a very quick return passage from Moreton Bay of 53 hours. Landing facilities along the river banks were primitive: wharves were not yet built and it was the practice of steamers to tie up to a tree. One such mooring point on the south bank of the Brisbane River, a log of 6 ft diameter, was known as "Macintyre's Gum Tree". A dispute with the owner induced the company to build a wharf in 1845. This was Brisbane's first wharf. A pioneer memorial park, now nearby, commemorates this event and the early growth of Brisbane.

Whaler *Emerald*

WHALERS CREATE NEW SETTLEMENTS

For many years past the whale ship has been the poineer in ferreting out the remotest and least well known parts of the earth. She had explored seas and archipelagoes which had no chart, where no Cook or Vancouver had ever sailed.

So wrote Herman Melville, author of *Moby Dick*, that classic American story of whaling. Of Australia he wrote:

After its first blunderborn discovery by a Dutchman, all other ships shunned these shores as pestiferously barbarous, but the whale ship touched there. The whale ship is the true mother of that now mighty colony.

Melville's claim may be exaggerated, but it is true that some of the hard-pressed early settlers saw salvation in a whale ship visit.

As early as 1791 the abundance of whales on the Australian coast was reported by convict ship captains. It was not long before these enterprising men, anxious to make a profitable return voyage after discharging their human cargo, refitted their ships for whaling. Europe was a hungry market.

Within a few years sealskin and whale oil formed Australia's first exports. In 1804 nine British ships were working on the New South Wales coast from Sydney. Van Diemen's Land and the Bass Strait islands followed quickly in development and soon the industry spread around the southern coastline and included small ports like Portland and Port Fairy in Victoria, Kangaroo Island in South Australia, and the Swan River and Albany in Western Australia. Later Eden in New South Wales became a well-known centre, being where Ben Boyd established his base.

It was all offshore work at first. Lookouts were posted on cliff tops and headlands, and from these points whaling oarsmen were signalled to the chase. It was also from these points that early townships grew. Indiscriminate hunting had destroyed seal populations but the wiser whale moved further out from the coast. The hunters followed. Men of many nationalities joined the chase in stout, specially built ships.

It was a French whaler captained by an Englishman that rescued the explorer Eyre and his Aboriginal companion Wylie on their long hot trek from Adelaide to Albany in 1841. The exhausted Eyre sighted the whaler

The American whaler Emerald *is shown here at an exciting moment of the chase, "hove to" to keep her on the spot in the long rolling seas of the Southern Ocean. Boats have been lowered away and crews are pulling eagerly towards the whale. The harpooner stands poised in the bow while the steersman skilfully uses sweep and rudder to put the little boat in an advantageous attacking position. Unlike the mother ship, these little boats were finely designed and built for speed and manoeuvrability. The pen sketch on the following page shows some features of this example of the boatbuilder's craft.*

Whaler *EMERALD*

anchored in a bay. A first-hand account is found in Eyre's own journal.

I now made smoke on a rock where I was and hailed the vessel upon which a boat was instantly put off and in a few moments I had the inexpressible pleasure of shaking hands with a fellow countryman, in the person of Captain Rossiter commanding the French whaler Mississippi. Our story was soon told and we were received with the greatest kindness and hospitality by the captain.

The bay is now named Rossiter Bay. Flinders had previously marked Lucky Bay in the vicinity.

By 1845 Sydney and Hobart had become thriving commercial centres for the industry at a time when Australia had very little produce to sell overseas. Ships of many nations, British, French, American, Spanish and Portuguese, called in to replenish stores and purchase or repair equipment such as flensing knives and harpoons, and sometimes to deal with agents to sell oil for transport to overseas markets.

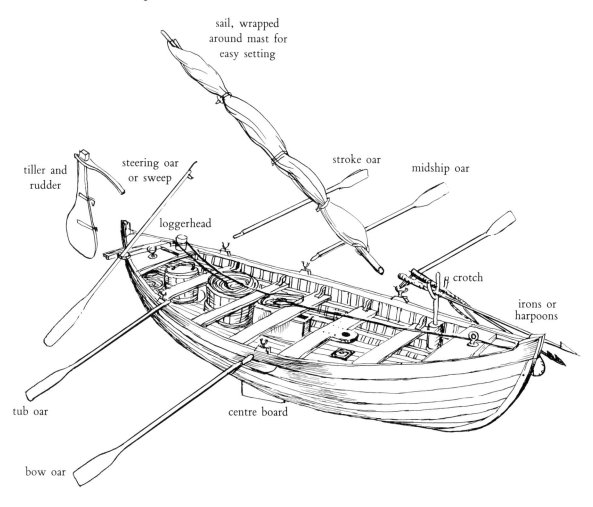

The nineteenth century whaleboat. These finely designed craft varied in length from 18 to 24 ft (5.5 to 7.3 m).

From 1844 to 1846 it is estimated that 300 American ships were whaling in Australian waters. One of these was the barque *Emerald* of 271 tons (275 t). She commenced working out of Salem, Massachusetts, in 1838. Two of her voyages, of four years each, brought her out to Australia, where she traded some of her oil in Hobart. On her last voyage in 1848 she was wrecked on the Isle of Madagascar.

The whaling captain was more than a good seaman—he had to be a good businessman. His ship was not large, and as a rule it was known for its sea-keeping qualities rather than for speed. The whaler was a lonely ship on wide waters. A ship going nowhere in particular, it had no cargo and no passengers to take from country to country. Its sole purpose was to search the seas where the sperm whale spouted. It bred hard and often homeless men, and crews included convicts, signed on in Australia; no questions were asked. Thirty-five to fifty men were crammed into a tiny forecastle or wherever a hammock could be slung.

Dame Mary Gilmore has recorded the grim story of one such seaman in her recollections, *Old Days, Old Ways*:

> On the whaling ships he saw the sea alive with whales; he saw men killed by brutal captains; he saw men forced to stand where the throw of the harpoon took them beyond their balance, and they went overboard with the throw; or by a slew of the boat were sawn in two by the racing rope; and he saw men driven under musket fire too soon near to the whale, so that the thrashing of the great flukes smashed the boats to splinters and the men were drowned with them. Of one boatload he was the only man left alive.

While great writers have eulogised the whalemen and their craft, it seems that the part their ships played in the early growth of Australia has been neglected.

Topsail Schooner *Wanderer*

BENJAMIN BOYD, AN EARLY ENTREPRENEUR

By 1841 the number of voluntary and willing immigrants and freeborn Australians had increased, reducing the proportion of convicts in the population. An optimistic outlook came to the face of the colony and a new social pattern was developing. Prosperous landowners and merchants were now able to afford the social pleasures of the home country and, for many this included the purchase of a yacht.

Anniversary Day, celebrating the founding of the colony, was an important feature of the social calendar. Sydney Harbour, a pleasant and most accessible playground, provided the setting and yachting races provided the main events of the day. So popular were these races that the day soon became known as Regatta Day in Hobart and Sydney.

In 1844 Commodore for the day in Sydney was Mr Benjamin Boyd. His flagship was the schooner *Wanderer*. But it was not simply for social purposes that Boyd had brought his yacht to Australia. Nor was he just another merchant adventurer dealing in freight, picking up a cargo here and selling it there. He was what would today be termed a financial magnate, and he intended to use his yacht for business as well as pleasure, for both of which purposes she was ideal. Her Royal Yacht Squadron burgee gave her an added status which attracted the attention of the right business and social contacts—persons of high standing and wealth.

Boyd, a London stockbroker, had been earlier inspired by reports of great new opportunities for big business in the colony. He proposed to combine sheep and cattle stations, whaling and shipping and related financial activities. To support this objective, two companies were formed, the Royal Bank of Australia and the Australian Wool Company. Three steamers were sent out laden with stores and equipment for the venture. Boyd followed in *Wanderer*.

She was a real yacht, in every sense of the word. She had been classified as an Admiralty yacht, a naval vessel used for ceremonial occasions. Sumptuously fitted out for a long cruise, she was armed with thirteen guns plus two ornamental ones for saluting purposes. (It was still assumed that pirates roamed the high seas.) Variously described as 240 odd tons, 141 tons net and 84 tons, her size is difficult to establish. The Royal Yacht Squadron at Cowes, England, where she was registered, cannot provide any more information and the model from which the painting was developed, now in the home of one of Boyd's descendants, gives no clear guide to the exact dimensions of the original but she was big—perhaps as much as 100 ft (31.5 m) long.

One source describes her as "a schooner of architectural proportions befitting a yacht, her hull low and black, her taut and tapering masts, her choice of ornaments, her luxurious accommodation and matchless sailing qualities, a

The painting shows Wanderer *under full sail in her original rig with the Royal Yacht Squadron ensign flying from her gaff and with sky and sea indicating a wind change. The* Seahorse *is in the distant cloud shadow.*

Topsail Schooner *WANDERER*

very fast sailing topsail schooner she had a flush deck, her cabins were fitted up with every possible attention to convenience and with great elegance."

With a picked crew and a former naval captain in command, Boyd left Plymouth in December 1841 and after what seems to have been a leisurely cruise calling at Rio, Tristan da Cunha, Cape Town and other interesting ports, he first called in at Port Phillip Bay before arriving in Port Jackson on 18 July 1842.

Leisure over, Boyd now went into action immediately. His steamer *Seahorse* went into service on 15 August taking passengers, sheep, cattle, horses and merchandise to Melbourne and Launceston. A regular service included Twofold Bay, where he was building a township for his whaling interests. Another of his vessels was *Juno*, the first steamer into Adelaide, South Australia. His third steamer *Cornucopia* worked the same routes, but was later chartered by the Government to assist with the settlement at Gladstone, Queensland. Business and pleasure took *Wanderer* to most of these ports.

Boyd's business activities extended beyond shipping. By 1844 he was one of Australia's biggest landholders. Boyd had come to Australia to establish a branch of the Royal Banking Company of London in which he held some interest and, on behalf of the shareholders, purchased properties in Queensland and New South Wales. Boyd Town on Twofold Bay, New South Wales, was planned to be an outlet for the produce of pastoral holdings as well as a whaling base. However, it appears that Boyd's ambitions were too big for the Australia of that time and speculating shareholders were impatient. By 1847 he was in financial difficulties. London shareholders voted him out of business, the assets were sold, and in 1849 Boyd Town was deserted. Boyd retained only the *Wanderer* and some land at Twofold Bay. The ultimate destiny of the *Seahorse*, *Juno* and *Cornucopia* is unclear.

Wanderer sailed from Sydney on 26 October 1849 with a melancholy Boyd on board, off to try his fortune on the Californian goldfields. This time there were no grand salutes or bunting to cheer *Wanderer* on her way as there had been on her arrival in Sydney in 1842. Moreover, it was a fruitless voyage and one that turned to disaster on the return. Boyd went ashore on the island of San Christobel and was never seen again, his crew later reporting that he had been killed by natives. *Wanderer* sailed on to Australia and was wrecked on the coast near Port Macquarie, and here *Wanderer*'s sad end was linked to our next story about a man who, unlike Boyd, started out with nothing but a gaol sentence yet ended his days in peace and prosperity and, ultimately, with civic distinction.

Although Boyd's imaginative business ventures failed, at least one benefit to Australia was the influx of migrants to work on his holdings in what is now known as the Eden-Monaro district of New South Wales.

Topsail Schooner *Elizabeth Cohen*

REGULAR SERVICE TO PORT MACQUARIE

A simple report in the *Shipping Gazette* of 6 December 1851, describing *Wanderer*'s demise, hides a story of significance belied by its brevity. It illuminates development along the coastline hardly mentioned in our history books and introduces a noteworthy individual, whose efforts added to the making of Australia. The report states:

> On Thursday 13th ultimo Mr. Benjamin Boyd's yacht the Wanderer *anchored off the bar at Port Macquarie and on the following morning a boat belonging to Messrs. Cohen and Company put off to ascertain if any communication was required with the shore. The crew found her in a disabled state, her main-mast and foremast both sprung above the deck as well as her jib-boom. They reported that Mr. Boyd had been killed by natives and they expressed a wish to enter Port Macquarie in order to get her repaired. Mr. Easton, master of the* Elizabeth Cohen, *advised that on account of her draft of water she should not come in, but subsequently went off with his crew to assist. Messrs. Cohen's bar boat was stove in, but they sent out their tug boat and at ebb-tide all the movables that is was possible to secure were got out and conveyed to Messrs. Cohen's store.*

Captain Easton was the pilot at Port Macquarie. The tugboat would have been a small paddle-steamer. Most of the sparse information we have about *Elizabeth Cohen* is recorded on the Sydney register, 1850, but she was built some time before this.

She was built on the Manning River, New South Wales. Her builders, Newton and Malcolm, enjoyed easy access to ample and appropriate timber: cedar, ironbark, blackbutt and flooded gum. The Manning River was a prolific shipbuilding district and over 110 ships of various sizes were built on the river banks before mid-century. *Elizabeth Cohen* was a typical product of this thriving region. Her dimensions were given as "43 tons measure", length 53 ft 7 ins (16.3 m), beam 15 ft (4.6 m), draught 6 ft 7 ins (2 m). She was small but beamy and shallow, and suited to her purpose, which included negotiating harbour bars.

This was a time when many of the attractive coastal areas, sighted from the sea but blocked by harsh bush behind, were being unlocked by settlers. Their main supplies came ashore on to the beaches. Then came the wharves and jetties. Henry Cohen of Messrs Cohen and Co. built one of the first wharves at Port Macquarie.

There was a lively trade in timber from the northern ports and many Sydney homes today boast beautiful red cedar from northern New South Wales. Cargoes varied: maize, hides, general merchandise, and always a few passengers making the trip between the north coast and Sydney "the easiest way". It was in fact the normal way to travel; packhorse and bullock cart were the only alternatives.

A first hand report of one such journey exists in *Annabella Boswell's Journal*, a contemporary account that is still in print today:

> *I quite well remember our return voyage to Sydney in November 1839. It was in a tiny sailing vessel called the* Elizabeth Cohen, *crowded with passengers, and sick and miserable we all were. Two people played cribbage loud*

PS Newcastle

⚓ *First sailing in 1882, the* Newcastle *was one of the last paddle steamers on the New South Wales coast.*
She was very popular with passengers on the run between Sydney, Newcastle and up river to Morpeth.
In 1924 she was sold to breakers and her hull scuttled outside Sydney Heads.

and long in the cabin off which our little den opened. I had never heard of the game, and wondered much what they could be talking about. The steward was a very superior man and very attentive to us; he was, in fact, part owner of the schooner, and when we arrived in Sydney late on Sunday evening, and no one came to meet us, he insisted on our going to his house for the night, and his nice, pretty little wife made us very comfortable.

Elizabeth Cohen plied busily and profitably in the service until October 1857, when she was last reported as "sighted off Broken Bay, New South Wales". Her owner, the remarkable Mr Henry Cohen, was a convict and a gentleman, who had a tailoring business and other interests in the Edgeware Road, London. Transported in 1832 on a charge of "being in possession of promissory notes", he was sentenced to fourteen years at Port Macquarie. He served seven years and apparently earned the admiration of the Governor, who owned a property some kilometres away from the gaol. He was allowed to take the bullock cart to town for stores and became the station's bookkeeper.

⚓ *Shown here* Elizabeth Cohen *battles a seething mountain of water that is typical when the black north wind blows along the New South Wales coast. Her topsail is coming in, her fore-sail and mainsails are shortened on the luff (the front edge of the sail) by a reef on the foot to ease pressure yet still keep enough force to steer her through the confused seas.*

Topsail Schooner *ELIZABETH COHEN*

His wife Elizabeth and eight children followed him out in 1833 as free migrants in the famous ship *Brothers*. They set up in business almost immediately on arrival in the Port Macquarie district and on his emancipation Henry was reunited with his family, joining an already established business, which grew quickly to ownership of a store and a hotel. The little schooner, named after his wife, was built to maintain supplies to these activities and to provide an outlet for local produce.

Henry established a wholesale grocery firm in George Street, Sydney, and to serve the interests of the north coast pioneers became one of the first shareholders of the North Coast Steamship Company. Messrs Cohen and Company thrived. Convict 33/3400 was one of those who threw off the stigma of a convict past and with grit and determination prospered by his efforts, showing a characteristic that we like to claim as Australian.

After the 1857 report *Elizabeth Cohen*, schooner, was never heard of again and was presumed lost during a sudden storm off the New South Wales coast.

Ship *Marco Polo*

A TIME OF GOLD AND IMMIGRATION

The clipper ship was a special class of sailing ship. With a fast fine-lined hull and three towering square-rigged masts, it developed between 1850 and 1860 and held the supremacy of sail for long ocean passages for many years against the rising challenge of steam.

Marco Polo was a famous member of that class. She was built in 1851 in New Brunswick, Canada, of Canadian softwood for export to Great Britain, and was bought by the enterprising Liverpool shipowner James Baines for his Black Ball Line.

The *London Illustrated News* in 1853 described her with enthusiasm: "Her lines fore and aft are beautifully fine, she had an entrance as sharp as a steamer and a bottom like a yacht, she has above water all the appearance of a frigate." Her measurements—length 184 ft (56 m), beam 36 ft 3 ins (11 m), hold depth 29 ft 4 ins (9 m) and gross tonnage 1665 tons (1692 t)—were by no means large for her class, but were large enough to make her ride more easily in big seas and allow some comfort to passengers, especially on the long run in the "roaring forties" to Australia.

Baines fitted her out for passengers with a standard of luxury unrivalled for first and intermediate class travellers and she even carried two doctors. In 1852 she made her maiden voyage from Mersey to Melbourne under the infamous Captain "Bully" Forbes, creating a record of sixty days. Her homeward journey around the Horn took seventy-six days.

A Melbourne shipping notice of 1854 advertised a sailing to Liverpool with passengers, gold and cargo of the celebrated and favourite clipper ship *Marco Polo* (1665 tons), Captain Wild, armed and fitted with bullion safes, this noble ship is now in Hobson's Bay, having landed over 700 passengers in good health, not withstanding that the voyage was unusually protracted for her, owing to an accident to her water tanks. Her three previous passages out and home including all the detention abroad, were accomplished in 17 months and 25 days, a feat never yet equalled by any steamer or sailing vessel and it is expected this passage home will fully equal previous achievements. The rates of passage money including a liberal dietary scale of the best provisions are: Saloon £80, second cabin £40, intermediate £25.

Within a period of less than two years, 1852 to 1854, Melbourne's population increased from 27 000 to 70 000: it was the Gold Rush time. Many of these newcomers would have made their passage on a ship of the Black Ball Line which catered especially for emigrant traffic to Australia.

The fleet had many ships that were later to become famous and included *Lightning* which, like *Marco Polo*, made more than 400 miles (640 km) in a day running the easterly down, that is, sailing from west to east in the forty degree south latitude. *Lightning* was destroyed by fire while loading wool in Geelong. *Sovereign of the Seas*, *Champion of the Seas* and others of the line all made a name for speed and popularity. The largest of the Black Ball

Line ships was the 288 ft (89 m) *Schonberg* which ultimately met its end when driven aground on the Victorian coast. This disaster signalled the end of the colourful career of her captain, "Bully" Forbes, a man noted for the brutality of his command which was felt by both passengers and crew.

During her period under Forbes' command, *Marco Polo* was celebrated in a song which used to be heard in the waterside pubs of Liverpool, Glasgow and Australia, and is still performed by a well-known Liverpool group.

THE MARCO POLO

The Marco Polo is a very fine ship, the fastest on the seas,
Australia's strand we soon will land, and "Bully" Forbes he's
*   gonna look for me.*
We'll jump this ship in Melbourne Town, and go a-digging
*   after gold,*
There's fortune there underneath the ground, where the
*   eucalyptus grows.*

The Black Ball owner Mister Payne, said to Captain Forbes
*   one day,*
It's up to you to keep your crew when the gold calls them
*   away.*
Said "Bully" Forbes to Mister Payne, I have a plan so fine,
Just leave it to me and you will agree, I'm the best in the
*   Black Ball Line.*

When we reached the Australian shore, "Bully" Forbes
*   declared the scurvy,*
There's a quarantine law and you cannot go ashore until we
*   reach the River Mersey.*
The call of gold in Ballarat was now burning in my mind,
And overboard I did prepare and swim to the other side.

But "Bully" Forbes had the Melbourne Peelers a-waiting on
*   the quay,*
And a crack on the head and a boot on the arse was the
*   fortune gained by me.*
And now I lie in the Salthouse Dock, I'll go to sea no more,
*   Sir.*
I've done me time with the Black Ball Line and the Captain
*   'Bully" Forbes, Sir.*

Chorus.
Marco Polo the fastest on the sea.
Marco Polo the fastest on the sea.

The melancholy lilt of the Irish-Scottish air is the essence of the melody. It was the period of famine in Ireland and the economic depression in Scotland and northern England when many migrants left the "old country" in search of freedom and the chance of a decent livelihood. They brought with them not only their songs but a spontaneous exuberance. Both were useful antidotes to misery.

⚓ *The painting shows* Marco Polo *in her more graceful days arriving in Port Phillip Bay. Her sail area is being reduced in sequence to slow her down and keep steerage way to allow the smoke-belching tug to take her to her moorings in Hobson's Bay. At her main mast head is the Black Ball Line house flag, her mizzen flies her identifying code, and the red ensign of Britain's merchant fleet streams out from her gaff. The black and white painted hull follows the traditional pattern of the old frigate gun ports.*

MARCO POLO

SS Great Britain

SS Great Britain, *designed by the famous British engineer Isambard Kingdom Brunel, incorporated many engineering innovations. She was the largest ship of the day to be built of iron, was screw propelled by a chain drive system and was the first ship to be divided into water tight compartments. Her maiden voyage was in 1845 from Merseyside, Liverpool, on the Atlantic run. Three years later she entered the Australian service and brought us many migrants—more than 600 on one voyage. She represented one of the earliest challenges to the supremacy of sail.*

SS Great Britain's auxiliary sail rig was also a departure from tradition, being fore and aft rigged on five of her six masts. In 1882 her engines were taken out and she was converted to sail, but storm damage at Cape Horn in 1886 forced her to shelter on the beach in the Falkland Islands. SS Great Britain remained in the Falklands until 1970 when her stout hull was towed back to her builder's yard in Bristol. She was restored and is now preserved in Britain as a museum. Her dimensions are 289 ft (88 m) long, 50 ft (15 m) wide with a gross tonnage of 3720 tons (3779 t).

An account of one memorable voyage of Great Britain *is preserved in* The Letters of Rachel Henning, *the diary of a woman who emigrated to Australia aboard this great liner in 1861. From on board the ship she wrote home to her sister in England:*

We had very rough weather during Tuesday and Wednesday, but still nothing remarkable, but yesterday morning it began to blow again, and for about six hours we had such a hurricane as no one on board ever saw before. To say that I never knew anything like it is nothing, but all the oldest sailors say a West Indian tornado was the only thing it was like.

Providentially it came by daylight; began about nine, and the worst was over by three. I could never give you the least idea of the force or roar of the wind, and some of the passengers who ventured on deck said the *Great Britain*, big as she is, looked like a cockleshell among the waves, and that it seemed impossible but she must be buried in them.

She behaved admirably, took in very little water, and came up as stiff as possible after every roll. Several seas came on board, however; one broke into the saloon and thence into the cabins, one of which was three feet deep in water. The steward mopped and dipped it out in buckets. Some water got into our cabin, and, on going in to investigate, I found that one of my boxes was standing in a puddle; and remembering that the children's likeness was at the bottom of that very box, I determined, gale or no gale, to unpack it and get the picture out, which I did.

As *Marco Polo* aged, her passages became slower because her timbers, like those of all softwood ships, became waterlogged but even in 1867 she sailed from Melbourne to Liverpool in seventy-six days, beating the steamer *Great Britain* by eight days. She continued in the Australian trade till 1871, when she was sold to a new owner to be employed as a general trader between Quebec and Europe. Canadian timber was one of her main cargoes. In 1883 she ran ashore on Prince Edward Island, Canada, and was a total loss.

The days of the wooden hull for large ships were drawing to a close. Later clippers, like *Cutty Sark*, were timber built over iron framing. Britain was then undergoing her Industrial Revolution and iron began to replace wood in most constructions. The fully iron-built steamers, like *Great Britain*, began to offer severe competition to the until then supremacy of sail. But sail was not to be outclassed easily. Steam had many years of tradition and experience to overtake and other problems to resolve before a new phase in this exciting period of marine transport could occur.

PS *Lady Augusta* & PS *Mary Ann*

OPENING UP THE INLAND

The land-seeking pioneers followed the explorers, turning away from the sea and spreading inland. They were confronted by a sombre ochre-coloured country, rough, unfriendly and often hostile. But through it all ran the rivers.

Australia's greatest river—the Murray—finds its way through three states, New South Wales, Victoria and South Australia, and many townships have grown on its banks. The opening up and commercial development of the region makes an exciting story for it started with a race. Its heroes were the only two contestants—Francis Cadell and William Randell.

Cadell arrived in Adelaide in 1848. On seeing the wide expanse of Lake Alexandrina at Goolwa on the mouth of the Murray, he envisaged a scene of steamer traffic taking stores to the outback and returning with wool, wheat and other produce to the coastal ports, thence to be transhipped to hungry overseas markets.

To prove the practicality of his ideas he paddled a boat made of beer barrel staves and canvas from Swan Hill to Goolwa and reported his findings to Governor Sir Henry Young so convincingly that a proclamation was issued: "Four thousand pounds to the first man to navigate a two foot draught steamer up river to the Murray–Darling Junction."

Cadell formed a company, acquired a suitable vessel in Sydney and sailed it down to Lake Alexandrina, where it was fitted out for its new function and renamed *Lady Augusta* in honour of the Governor's wife. Sir Henry asked that he, together with his wife and entourage, be taken on the trip, and so more time was spent in constructing appropriate facilities on board. Eventually in August 1853 Captain Cadell set the wheels turning and headed upstream.

Day after day under blue spring skies and golden evenings the river reached ahead. Ducks and swans scattered at *Lady Augusta*'s approach and provided many a meal for the dining saloon. The blissful trippers knew nothing of what excitement lay ahead. For there was competition—in the form of Captain Randell in his *Mary Ann*.

Randell had come to Australia as a boy in 1837 with his family, who settled at Lake Victoria on the lower Murray. He shared the same ideas about navigation and trade along the Murray as Captain Cadell and when he heard

Lady Augusta is shown as fitted out for her first voyage, with two funnels and a long deckhouse. To avoid overhanging branches and enable easier navigation of the upper reaches of the winding river, the deckhouses and one engine and funnel were later removed. Her practical career continued for many years. The Mary Ann is seen drawn up to the river bank where she is taking on timber to fire her boilers.

PS *LADY AUGUSTA* and PS *MARY ANN*

of the proclamation he got to work immediately. It was most likely that he had never seen a steamship, but with the true bushman's inventive resourcefulness he built and launched the little 20 ton steamer at Mannum in 1853. Like Cadell he was completely unaware of a rival and, confident that he had the river all to himself, set off on a leisurely cruise. He was upriver, well ahead.

But this lead was soon to be challenged and Randell aboard the *Mary Ann* recorded the moment when his competitor arrived on the scene.

> *We were now within three days' journey of Swan Hill, and after having moored the boat at the bank of the river, and gone to rest, we were awakened by an unusual noise upon the water, and when we turned out to ascertain the cause of the commotion we beheld the* Lady Augusta, *steaming up the river at the rate of three or four knots.*
> *It was then near eleven o'clock at night, and although our sleep had been disturbed, we followed in a few hours, and passed her again next morning.*

The leisurely progression of both boats was at an end. Boilers were stoked to give maximum speed and the cruise became a race. The steamers passed and repassed one another many times. When one stopped to cut wood for fuel the other would thump ahead. Every pound of steam pressure and every ounce of helmsmanship added to the excitement, but slowly the bigger vessel drew ahead.

Lady Augusta reached Swan Hill in the evening of 17 September 1853, and while congratulations were being extended and toasts drunk at a typical backblocks welcome in Rutherford's public house the little *Mary Ann* steamed around the last bend. It turned into a jolly evening, and by mutual consent Swan Hill was declared the finishing line.

Cadell won his four thousand pounds, and the Government of South Australia also rewarded Randell with three hundred pounds, which was supplemented by a public subscription of seven hundred pounds. *Mary Ann* pressed on to what is now the famous port of Echuca and both returned to Goolwa, embarking shearers and picking up bales of wool and other produce on the way.

Following this event it was realised that the smooth expanse of the rivers provided a quicker and better highway than the bumpy ruts of a wagon track and within a few years regular traffic as far as the Darling Junction and beyond began. The thump-thud of paddles and the steamer's blast on the silent stream were music to the lonely settlers. Many books have been written on this romantic chapter of Australian history.

In one of them, *River Boats* by Ian Mudie, there is included the reminiscences of one grateful riversider who remembered the arrival of the *Lady Augusta* and the change the river boats made to life along the Murray:

> *No teams had been up, or down, for two years. There were two seasons' wool stored in the sheds; the remaining flour was awfully musty; boots, saddlery, tinware, "slops," and the like had, long since, given out in the store.*
> *I remember we used to boil "fat hen" (a weed which resembles dandelion) for vegetables, and we bore the musty flour as best we could, when, presto! all the muddle came to an end . . . The two years' siege was raised. Fifty pound bags of pure white flour, fresh from the mills of Adelaide, spick and span boxes of loaf sugar, and equally spick and span cases of Van Martell's brandy, and sperm candles also clean; and other goods too numerous to mention. Not covered with the mud and dust of 800 miles of bush travel; not doled out in occasional dray-loads of 30 cwt. at a time, but fresh and clean only a week ago from the Adelaide stores . . . Here was a metamorphosis with a vengeance, and the congested wool stores soon afforded ample return loading for the steamer and her barge.*

Cadell and Randell are well remembered in the riverbank towns.

PS *Adelaide*

TIMBER IN TOW

An important sequel to the contest between Cadell and Randell was the genesis of one of Australia's richest agricultural areas. The nourishment of trade and commerce made possible by the river boats fostered many new settlements and soon the silent river became part of a busy thoroughfare that reached out along the Murrumbidgee and Darling Rivers and other Murray tributaries and through three states: South Australia, Victoria and New South Wales.

Cadell and Randell acquired more steamers, naming some of them after the new townships they served—*Albury* built in 1855 and *Gundagai* built in 1858 were just two of many others. Randell set up a drydock at Mannum to build ships for other owner-skippers and all along the river building slipways bloomed.

Many types of ship were tried. Two Americans, Murrey and Jackson, brought out their sternwheelers, Mississippi type paddle-wheelers, but these proved unsuitable because of sandbanks and shallows in the dry season, or heavy snags and fallen trees floating just below the surface in the wet season; the sidewheeler simply rode over these hazards.

Trade upriver was generally in flour, tea, sugar, clothing, pots and pans and other domestic and farming equipment; downriver it was in wool and other produce to be transhipped to the clippers awaiting cargo at Adelaide. Nearly every trip, up and down, carried shearers and other passengers who enlivened the life of the townships, as well as enriching the publicans' pockets en route. The church also took its ministry along the river in the little steamer *Etona*: christenings and weddings and other services were performed and quite a unique way of life developed.

William Drage, who was christened on the old *Etona*, gives this description of those days in his book *River Boats and River Men*.

We river kids could tell you the name of any steamboat on the river long before she hove in sight around the bend. More than fifty boats were working the rivers when I was growing up before the first World War, and we knew all about them. A lad would look up from his fishing line and say, "I reckon that's the Mannum *coming," or the* Marion, *or* Industry, *or whatever she might be. As soon as we heard a steamboat plugging along, we knew her name. The engines and paddles of each boat, and of course her whistle when she blew a couple of blasts, made a distinctive music. Very often we could tell whether she was light ship or loaded, or whether she was towing a barge or two, just by the sounds. We didn't know how we knew: we'd simply absorbed it because steamboats were a big part of our busy and adventurous lives. We took in the knowledge through our skins, by hanging around the wharves when the steamboats were loading, and watching them pass by, and listening to the adults talk about them. We knew the names of their skippers and cooks and engineers, and probably a good many of their crewmen, too. And if we didn't happen to know these men personally then there was still a good chance that we knew all about them, on account of the stories passed up and down the river.*

I was a river lad from the moment I was born at Renmark on the Murray River, on 30 May 1901. I was even christened aboard a steamboat: the old Etona *that was run by the Church of England as a mission steamer to visit the little settlements along the river. She was fitted up with a chapel by Archdeacon Bussell in 1903 or thereabouts, and replaced the mission steamer* Glad Tidings.

No permanent charts of the meandering rivers could be produced, as charts needed to be changed whenever the seasons affected the river's course. For navigation some skippers devised and produced their own charts suitable to the peculiarities of their vessels. These charts consisted of a length of oiled linen about 45 cm wide and about 4.5 m long on which the bends and hazards, such as sandbanks, projecting tree roots and so on, were marked as they were passed. The linen strip was mounted on a roller, a turn of which brought up the next section of the route ahead. *Adelaide* carried one such chart.

In 1855 ex-convict Henry Hopwood, a bright young lad from Lancashire via the convict settlement of Van Diemen's Land, operated a punt across the river 1065 miles (1702.5 km) from the sea. This became a focal point for the local farmers and from such a small enterprise grew the town of Echuca. By 1872 this had become Victoria's second largest port—a rollicking town. The area was rich in red gum, a hard timber suitable for heavy use such as railway sleepers. The task of getting the timber out fell largely to the lot of PS *Adelaide*.

PS *Adelaide* was built for passengers and general cargo in 1866 for Officer & Grassie Co. of Poon Boon and Murray Downs station (a showplace today), but was later adapted to tow timber barges for the sawmills of Echuca. Her hull, 76 ft (23 m) long and 17 ft (5.2 m) wide, was shaped in three-inch thick red gum planking on an iron frame. Her 14 ft (4.3 m) diameter paddles were turned by a two-cylinder steam engine fuelled on sawmill offcuts. Echuca was her working base.

She continued her task well into the twentieth century, until the roads and railways she helped to build rendered her services no longer necessary. Like many of her company she was left to decay on the river bank—the Murray's backwaters still hold relics of the "old-timers"—but happily, thanks to the enthusiasm of voluntary groups interested in Australia's past, she was brought ashore to rest in Hopwoods Gardens, Echuca. Here paddleboat lovers restored her to healthy working condition.

Now together with *Pevensy*, *Marion*, the old mission ship *Etona* and some other "old-timers" she cheerily churns Murray River waters and proudly toots her steam whistle for the enjoyment of tourists and holiday makers. Even the old wharves and hotels of Echuca are being preserved to provide a stirring picture of that exciting phase of Australia's growth.

The painting shows Adelaide *rounding an upriver bend in the dry season. In the spring, when the river is high in flood, heavy fallen trees like those in the foreground would float into her path but her shape and stout construction would push them aside. The tall, well-stayed mast, amidships just behind the wheelhouse, was the towing point, enabling the towline to clear any deck cargo on the stern, and the tall pole in the bow served to help the helmsman to see his "pointing" when the bow was obscured by foredeck cargo.*

PS *ADELAIDE*

SS *Despatch*

GIPPSLAND'S LIFELINE

The years from 1860 onwards witnessed a period of transition in all modes of transport all the world over, and most of the changes were to be seen in shipbuilding. Wooden hulls and masts with canvas to collect power gave way to iron hulls and masts, steel wire rigging and coal for power. The disadvantages of steam power—the space occupied by engines, boilers and coal bunkers, space that in a sailing ship would have cash-earning capacity, and the fact that the power was not free—were being overcome by engineers.

There were improvements in the compound engine, and there was the later development of the triple expansion engine which turned a propeller and replaced the cumbrous paddlewheels of the early steamer. As well newly designed boilers and furnaces reduced the quantity of coal consumption. Other refinements meant fewer men on deck but more below. All this liberated the ship from dependence on the winds and made it easy to maintain a regular timetabled service. It spelt out the decline of the cutters, ketches, schooners, brigs and brigantines that had pioneered the sea lanes of Australia, establishing small ports in the service of the early settlers.

At first the early steamship followed the traditional lines of the sailing ship. Then a new shape developed over many years of experience with the sea, but sail was still carried "just in case". Seamen were "belt and braces" men, basically conservative. The new ship shape was the work of unsentimental and sometimes overconfident engineers. The elegant clipper, or fiddle bow, was gradually being replaced by the straight stem, the "front end". There was no need for the helmsman to watch the sail trim, so the steering control could now be located amidships, a drier position, and the bridge took the importance of the poop. The tall slim funnel was purely practical: it increased the furnace draught.

SS *Despatch* was a typical example of the time and one of the best known of many traders working along the coast of Victoria. She was built in Scotland in 1869 for the Parker Company, which later became the Huddart Parker Steam Ship Company. She was 151 ft (46 m) long, 20 ft (6 m) wide and 10 ft (3 m) deep "in the hold". Under schooner rig she sailed out from Britain via Cape of Good Hope and commenced service on Port Phillip Bay to Melbourne, Portarlington and Geelong. After seven profitable years she was used by the Victorian Government as a tender for the coastal lighthouses and other navigation marks—a vital, newly realised duty to safety at sea which she served for over three years.

To the east of Melbourne lies the rich pastoral district of Gippsland, which includes the famous Gippsland Lakes, divided from the sea by a narrow strip of sand dunes and shifting entrances. When a new engineered entrance was opened on 18 January 1889, Bairnsdale boomed as a centre for the whole of Gippsland. *Despatch* entered into

SS Despatch *is shown "fires down" steaming sedately in the calm sheltered waters of the Lakes.*

SS *DESPATCH*

trade in the region. The lakes are fed by two rivers navigable to small paddle-steamers. These craft would pull into the river bank almost opposite the farmer's front door and load or unload whatever cargo was required or offered. The cargo was then taken into storage at Bairnsdale wharf to be collected by *Despatch* weekly for delivery in Melbourne. Cargo from Melbourne would be left for distribution to the farmers and stores by the little river steamers.

Despatch used to leave her berth on the Yarra River, near what is now Queen's Bridge, every Saturday at noon. She called in at Port Albert to collect or deliver cargo and would arrive at Bairnsdale wharf early on Tuesday morning. Here her few passengers disembarked and general cargo for the entire district was unloaded. After loading wool, maize, hops, the famous cheeses of Gippsland, quartz from upcountry mines and whatever else was offering—quite a mixed cargo—she would depart on the Thursday morning.

The railways reached Bairnsdale in 1888 but the seaways continued as the main traffic lines for many years. *Despatch* maintained her service with the regularity of a grocery run well into the twentieth century. It was a creditable performance considering the poor harbour conditions and bumping sand bars at Port Albert or at Waratah Bay. When the southerly came up out of Bass Strait she had to get away from the jetty; when prevented by that vicious wind from leaving shelter, she stayed in harbour. Her crew would bide time by a spot of fishing.

Despatch had a few minor accidents but never lost a man. In one in 1903, she hit the pier at Lakes Entrance and came off with little damage. However in 1911, after over twenty years of service to Gippsland's growing community, she did meet her end. While standing off the entrance awaiting an abatement of the heavy weather, it was discovered that her coal stocks were getting dangerously low. Her captain decided to make a run for it but *Despatch* was pushed by the seas onto some old piles at the entrance to the channel near Eastern Pier. She was badly holed and sank quickly but no lives were lost.

The Trading Ketches

SOUTH AUSTRALIA EXPANDS

North, south and westward from Sydney the spread of settlement grew. To Tasmania, to Victoria, to Queensland and then, following the tracks of the whalers and sealers, to South Australia (officially founded in 1836), came the new pastoral settlers. Most came by sea and at first they did not move far inland. Soon wool, wheat and copper came to be the export products, and South Australia began to thrive.

Except for Boston Bay, Port Lincoln, named by Flinders, there are not many good natural harbours in the long 3800 kilometre coastline of South Australia. The longest sections are the Spencer and St Vincent Gulfs and from these shores the colony grew. Local produce could be carted down to the beach to be loaded on to flat-bottomed barges and then taken out to the holds of the clipper ships at anchor in deeper waters.

Couta Boats

Named for their original use, barracouta fishing, couta boats crowded Victoria's small harbours early this century. These distinctive boats were well suited to their work, ranging in size from 18 to 25 ft (6 to 8 m) long and beamy for stability, but shallow in depth to enable rowing when necessary. They also had a wide, flat transom stern from which fishing lines could be easily trailed, a rising foredeck to keep dry and wide side decks to work on. Some were lug-sailed while others were gaff-rigged. Pictured is a Queenscliff boat in her local blue colours. Couta boats are still in use, but these days the same stout hulls are engine driven.

The Pearling Lugger

Pearling started in the 1870s with Australian Aborigines and Torres Strait Islanders working in shallow waters. As the industry grew, Japanese divers began to dominate and a specialised design—the pearling lugger—developed. The so-called lugger was, in fact, a 35 to 50 ft (13.7 to 15.3 m) gaff-rigged ketch or schooner that was roomy enough to accommodate divers as well as crew and able to work further out to sea than previous pearling boats. Two types evolved—the Thursday Island lugger and the Western Australian luggers which operated from Broome. One of the latter is shown sitting on the mud at low tide in Broome Harbour.

Trading Ketches MAY QUEEN and ONE AND ALL

A new type of vessel evolved to meet the new conditions. It had to be able to load from the beach and to work the tides through shallow waters and sand flats to otherwise inaccessible points of production, as well as to be able to sail across rough waters such as the notorious Backstairs Passage between the southern end of Yorke Peninsula and St Vincent Gulf and the stretch between Kangaroo Island and Spencer Gulf.

This vessel was simply called the ketch. Port Adelaide became the centre of a wide web of routes, which included Wallaroo and also Port Pirie for minerals and Port Augusta and Port Lincoln for grain. Ketches brought stone for the building of the growing city of Adelaide, and sailed south for sheep and other products to townships such as Robe. Timber they brought from Tasmanian ports, where most of these little ships had been built.

As well as bringing the tools of sustenance to the settlers, they performed the equally valuable function of social linkage and intercourse. The deck was a meeting place for passengers from the isolated communities. It was easier to travel to townships by sea. The ketches became part of the life of the districts. They provided some of the excitement of Saturday afternoon with racing for prizes, donated by the local hotel owners and business houses. They dominated Regatta Day events well into the twentieth century.

Briefly, the ketch, like the famous Thames barge, the couta boat of Victoria or the pearling luggers from the north-west coast of Australia, is a simple economic solution to a problem. Its sail area is divided on the two masts, mizzen being shorter than main to allow quick handling by the small crew, which rarely consisted of more than two men and a boy. The long bowsprit could slide inboard for crowded harbours. She had a shallow hull and a good beam but to hold a good grip on deeper open water she was fitted with a heavy centreboard. The length varied between 55 ft (17 m) and 65 ft (20 m) but she could carry 100 tons of cargo. How many semitrailers would that require today? She never needed a tug, and like all small ships she acquired an individuality reflecting the personality of her owners. The proud skipper would often "show off" and demonstrate his skill by putting on a show for the benefit of watchers. With all sail on, in a fresh breeze, he would approach a pier or the wall of a ship's hull, to the consternation of spectators expecting a crunch. At the last moment he would "round up"; the crew would coolly drop sail and the little ship would ease serenely alongside without a scrape. To watch these boats come in was an occasion, an outing for the family.

Family ownership and loving care kept some of these unique and versatile craft in service for many years. It is only in fairly recent years, that we have lost, through neglect, the old *Huon Chief*, a magnificent old ketch which for years lay rotting in the Derwent River, Hobart.

May Queen is still with us. She is 65 ft 8 ins (20 m) long, and 18 ft (5.5 m) beam and fully loaded draws only 5 ft (1.5 m) water. She was built at Franklin on the Huon River, Tasmania in 1867, of blue gum and stringy bark, and her timbers are still sound. She carried varied local produce, but timber was her main cargo; she averaged 25 000 ft per week during her long engagement in the Huon River traffic, a short but often rough trip through Storm Bay at the Derwent River mouth.

Shallow waters over a clear sandy bottom produce a distinctively coloured sea. Pictured in such waters are the South Australian ketch One and All *(with the black hull, sailing "off the wind" in the distance), built in 1878, lost in the Pacific in 1973; and (in the foreground, with the smart white hull, sailing a "beam wind") the Tasmanian ketch* May Queen.

Eventually, by 1860, but not without pressure from local citizenry, a few long jetties were built. A jetty meant a port, a centre for collection and distribution of cargoes, ultimately a township.

It was timber and the work of these little ships which built the jetties and also provided the sleepers for the railways. Both jetties and railways allowed for the expansion of South Australian settlements and their spread further inland, which led to greater production and in turn increased traffic to the ports. So Australia grew.

May Queen ceased trading in 1973 at the ripe old age of 106 years. In recent years she has acted as an Anniversary Day flagship at the Regatta on the Derwent River. She is still afloat and in good condition, thanks to the good care of the Hobart Marine Board and the wise decision of the Tasmanian Government of the day.

Barque Scottish Bard

MIGRANTS TO QUEENSLAND

It was the low cost of sail power and the all-paying hold capacity that kept the wind ship in service until the early twentieth century, especially on long voyages. While steam was consolidating its success along the shorter coastal routes and some overseas passengers were enjoying the luxury of the steamer and the faster passage allowed by the newly built Suez Canal, sail was assuming a humbler role. Coastal cargoes carried by sail were mainly timber, stone for building and coal to the main ports to feed the steamers. The glamour of the clipper ship era had passed but sail was not driven off the seas. For many years the cold side of the captain's nose and the action of the seabird upwind or downwind continued to be the indicators of a source of power obtainable at no cost, but to be used with care.

However very few of the great sailing ships remained to bring passengers from the old world. The gold rush had subsided and more skilled tradesmen and unskilled workers were sorely needed in the new areas developing away from the capital cities. The colonial governments established free and assisted migration schemes which made it easier for the less affluent to make their homes in the new country.

They were stalwart men and women, to whom the hardship of the long voyage under sail was an improvement on the misery of slum life in Dickensian England or the depressed existence of the poor of Ireland and Scotland. They endured the tough tradition of migration under sail in ships that were smaller and less spectacular than the old full-rigged clipper ships. These were barques, vessels whose rig was easier to handle and who thus needed a smaller crew than the old full-rigged ships had required.

In 1875 the colonial government of Queensland let out a contract for the carriage of migrants to ports north of Maryborough. This was awarded to a newly formed company, McIlwraith McEacharn, who built a fleet of eight barques for the purpose. These were *Scottish Bard* of 859 tons (873 t), *Scottish Hero* of 920 tons (935 t), *Scottish Knight* of 916 tons (930 t), *Scottish Lassie* of 899 tons (913 t), *Scottish Admiral* of 986 tons (1002 t), *Scottish Prince* of 950 tons (965 t), *Sir William Wallace* of 968 tons (983 t) and the largest of them all was *Scottish Wizard* of 1209 tons (1228 t). The company was called the Scottish Line.

Their first vessel, built in 1876 was the *Scottish Bard*. An interesting report in the *Central Queensland Herald* of 8 September 1877 throws an amusing light on this traffic.

> The barque Scottish Bard *sailed from Gravesend 18 May bound for Queensland having on board 254 souls equal to 225 statute adults and arrived safely at Townsville on 20 August 1877. The nationalities of the migrants is as follows: 130 English, 16 Scots, 107 Irish and 1 from a foreign country. Social conditions: 92 single men, 60 single women, 26 married men, 29 married women, 42 children between the ages of 12 to 1 and 7 infants. There were 9 full paying, 69 assisted, 154 free, 21 remittance and 1 free nomination. Occupations: 50 female domestic servants, 72 farm labourers, 19 labourers, 1 engine driver, 2 gardeners, 1 engineer, 1 miner, 2 tailors, 1 blacksmith, 2 painters, 1 mason, 1 sawyer, 2 carpenters and 2 others.*

Barque *SCOTTISH BARD*

Other "cargo" listed included picks and shovels and other building materials. Harbours did not exist up north and migrants were brought ashore in small boats and landed on the beach. It was not an easy landing.

The last ship of the Scottish Line built in 1881 was *Scottish Wizard*. A local newspaper reported:

A pleasant surprise was experienced on Thursday afternoon 26 January 1882 when the arrival of Scottish Wizard *barque, with immigrants from Maryborough was known, the vessel not being expected for a week or 10 days. She left Plymouth on 27 October and has made a fine passage of 91 days. Captain Scales reports by telegraph from Maryborough that all are well on board and no deaths occurred. The passengers on leaving Plymouth numbered 272, the number on arrival being increased by 2 births during the voyage.*

Her cargo included steel rails for the Maryborough–Bundaberg line then under construction, which was to accelerate inland developments.

When the migrant contract was completed these and the rest of the fleet of eight barques carried cargo only. *Scottish Bard* was sold to a Danish owner in 1894, was renamed *Thor*, and was lost at sea in 1900. *Scottish Wizard* was sold to Italian owners and renamed *Pasquale Lauro*; she was listed in 1917 as "missing, presumed lost". All were similarly accounted for.

There were many such vessels working well into the early twentieth century, "doing their bit" modestly and without fanfare. Unless involved in some dramatic event, they passed unsung and often left no other records than the ship's birth certificate, its registration number.

When their working life concluded, they were sold for scrap iron, left to decay in some backwater or submitted to the indignity of becoming coaling hulks to serve their noisy, smoke-belching successors. At least one example has been saved: Melbourne has lovingly restored *Polly Woodside* to do her bit in her old age as a maritime museum.

The painting shows Scottish Bard, *taking in royals before a short sharp squall, something frequently met in north Queensland waters. The house flag, Red Lion rampant on yellow ground, flying at her main masthead, in later years flew over a distinguished fleet of steamers.*

Ship *Loch Ard*

A DISASTROUS WRECK THAT BENEFITED SHIPPING

Along the rugged coastline of western Victoria between Warrnambool and Cape Otway is a spectacular cliff formation named Loch Ard Gorge. It commemorates a shipwreck that had more than enough dramatic and colourful detail for the most romantic novelist. The tragic event of 1 June 1878 also highlighted the basic advantage of steam over sail.

The Clyde-built iron ship *Loch Ard* was a handsome vessel of 1693 tons (1720 t), 262 ft (79.9 m) long and 38 ft (11.6 m) wide, with a depth of 24 ft (7.3 m). Her masts were over 150 ft (46 m) high. Misfortune struck early in her career when, despite her iron masts and steel standing rigging, she was dismasted in a gale. *Loch Ard* limped into port under jury rig. Three other ships foundered in the same storm.

When *Loch Ard* sailed from Gravesend on 2 March 1878 her new young captain had been married for only a few weeks; her previous captains had both died within a short period of each other. She had seventeen passengers, a crew of thirty-six and a mixed cargo on board.

The voyage was slow and uneventful until 31 May. Then, as *Loch Ard* was approaching the western entrance to Bass Strait, a rising sea fog obscured the sun, rendering both sextant and landfall sighting difficult, and even confusing the sounds used by mariners to navigate a coastline poorly marked by lighthouses.

Her captain had posted a lookout aloft as was usual practice under these conditions. At about 4 a.m. the lookout sighted cliffs towering above the mist and called out that he also heard breakers ahead.

The light wind was onshore and an onshore current exacerbated the difficulties. Without space or time to complete the complex manoeuvre of "going about", anchors were dropped but this was of no avail. *Loch Ard* struck a ledge of rock at the cliff base and her masts and spars brought boulders crashing down to the decks. Before dawn broke, helpless and badly holed, she slipped off the ledge and sank. It was a tragic shipwreck, but only one of many claimed by this rugged coast. Remarkably two souls survived this catastrophe. They were Eva Carmichael, a young lady passenger, and the young apprentice seaman Tom Pearce. The evidence they gave at the subsequent inquiry, according to the Melbourne *Argus* and other newspapers of that time, revealed an unusual story worth repeating.

As the ship broke up, the wreckage followed the sea current into the gorge. To this clung terrified men, women and children, trapped between vertical cliffs and the surging sea. At daylight Tom Pearce slipped from his upturned smashed boat, swam ashore to the flotsam-piled beach and found a large cave.

The same current that had swept Tom through the narrow entrance to the gorge brought Miss Carmichael,

Loch Ard is here shown approaching Bass Strait waters under a southern sky which often precedes a foggy morning.

LOCH ARD

clinging to wreckage. Tom heard her cry and, despite his weakness from abrasions and exhaustion, he swam out and brought her ashore through the dangerous drifting wreckage and carried her to the cave shelter. Her only clothing was a torn nightgown.

In Eva's words, according to newspaper reports,

He took me into a wild looking cave a few hundred yards from the beach, finding a case of brandy, broke a bottle and made me swallow some, which revived me. He pulled some shrubs and grass for me to lie on. I soon sank into a state of unconsciousness and must have remained so for hours.

Tom also had "a nip", rested a while and then with Eva fast asleep, climbed the steep cliff out of the gorge in search of help. In his own words, as reported, "when I got to the top my heart sank as I could not see anything resembling a settlement. The thought of Miss Carmichael lying in the cave made me make the effort to get help but having no boots on, progress was slow."

Happily Tom was noticed by some mustering horsemen and rescue was effected though Eva had wandered off from the cave when Tom returned with help and she had to be searched for in the scrub at the base of the cliff. Later, when news of the wreck became widespread, the Victorian public were greatly moved by Tom's bravery and raised a fund at the Melbourne Town Hall. He was also awarded the Royal Humane Society medal. The press made much of the survivors' story and predicted a lasting relationship but, to the disappointment of the romantics, Tom and Eva went their own separate ways.

Very little was recovered from *Loch Ard*'s deeply laden holds but a carefully packed porcelain peacock, Minton ware, 150 centimetres high, destined for exhibition in Sydney was washed ashore. It now rests in the Warrnambool Maritime Museum.

Hugh Gibson, who had been with the rescue party, described the tragic beach scene a day after the wreck.

I went down next morning at daylight and found a great accumulation of wreckage. The beach at the gorge I would say was 300 yards long from cliff to cliff, and there was a barricade at least eight feet high, right across, consisting of ship's cargo, which comprised commodities of all descriptions. You could not name an article of commerce that was not there. The barrier of wreckage contained goods of every conceivable description. There were pianos, concertinas, piece goods, ladies' dresses, candles, brandy and spirits, champagne, strychnine, telegraph instruments, etc. These were all at the foot of a gorge accessible only at one spot, and so, to a certain extent, secure from wreckers. I did not stay long that morning as there was only one harmless man there, a local resident. As for the ship, she was out of sight many fathoms deep, but there was a piece of spar hanging on the base of the cliff, with the reflection of sail below the water that marked the place where she had foundered. She was lost on an inaccessible island close to the mainland ... I went down again in the afternoon, and then found Mrs and Miss Ruby Carmichael, who had been washed ashore with lifebelts on, and pulled them above high water mark, covering them with calico we found among the wreckage. They were fully clothed and had not a scratch on them.

The sad flotsam of many such wrecks was found along that inhospitable coastline. Adding to the tragedy, numbered among them was *Napier*, the steamer chartered for salvage work on the *Loch Ard*.

The part played by *Loch Ard* in the shaping of Australia is greater than that of providing a romantic story or a name on the map. She demonstrated the responsibilities and limitations of a captain in sail. A steamer in the same circumstances would simply go astern or bring the rudder over and steam away from danger, but under sail sea room was needed to turn the ship around, especially if it was a large ship with a small crew. While the wreck of the *Loch Ard* caused the lighthouse service to be improved, it was a service that was to ultimately benefit a different kind of vessel, for the period of sail in shipping history was then drawing to a close. A new phase, the "big liner" era, was beginning.

Inscription on
Stone Above Loch Ard Gorge

*"Shall Not the Judge of all the Earth
do Right"
Sacred to the Memory of
Mrs. Evory Carmichael
and
Miss Ruby Carmichael
Whose bodies lie Beneath
also
In Remembrance of
Doctor Evory Carmichael
Misses Margaret and Annie
Carmichael
Master Evory and Thomas
Carmichael
All of Whom were lost in the Calamitous
Wreck of the "Loch Ard"
Saturday 1st June 1878
This stone is erected by Eva and William
Carmichael
The former of Whom
was most Miraculously preserved.
In affectionate Remembrance
of
Their Deceased Brothers and
Sisters.*

SS *Orient*

The loss of *Loch Ard* happened in a particularly disastrous period of shipwrecks, but it was this black period that excited concern and accelerated the new era of sea travel. Steam power became firmly established; the screw propeller superseded the clumsy paddle boxes; engines improved, producing more power per ton of coal; and new acts of parliament governing conditions at sea were passed. All these things contributed to a great reduction in the hardships and hazards of sea voyages.

The rush for gold had settled down, and within a few years agriculture and the export of meat, wheat and wool were establishing a new pattern of trade. Australia was expanding its growth radiating from each of the capital cities, all of which were seaports. To support and stimulate all this, migrants were needed. They came and, thanks to

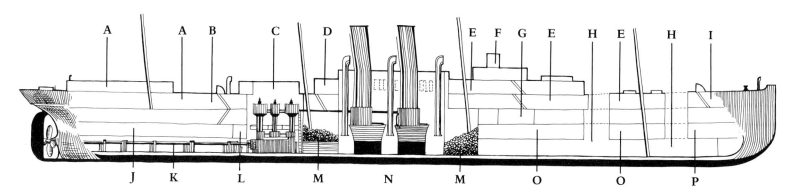

Cut-away of the Orient *showing the main accommodation and working areas.*

A. Second class passengers.
B. Steerage class passengers.
C. Engine room with skylight over 3 cylinder compound engine.
D. Engineer officers. Other engine room staff—stokers, greasers etc.—located in adjacent areas.
E. First class passengers.

F. Captain's bridge.
G. Galley. Cooks, stewards and other catering staff located in adjacent areas.
H. Hatches to cargo hold.
I. Seamen's quarters—the foc'sle.
J. Food and refrigerated storage.

K. Propeller shaft in tunnel.
L. Refrigeration machinery room.
M. Coal bunker, with tunnel to engine room.
N. Stokehold.
O. Cargo holds.
P. Stores—with anchor chain locker.

SS Orient is pictured passing through the Suez Canal on one of her early return trips to Britain. The yards crossing the foremast and mainmast were removed when she was rerigged on her first refit. Confidence in engines was by then complete.

SS ORIENT

RMS Ormonde

⚓ *This long-serving Orient liner with accommodation for 1500 passengers brought many migrants to Australia. Built in 1918,
she served as a troopship during both world wars. She returned to normal service in 1947, but was finally broken up in 1952 in Scotland.*

the skills of the engineers (mainly Scots) and the competition between the new shipowners to attract passengers, they even found the forty days' passage out pleasurable.

SS *Orient* was the first steamship built specially for a regular Australian service. Her owners, the Orient Steam Navigation Company, had operated a mail-carrying steamer as early as 1851 but SS *Orient* set a new standard.

Built in 1879, she was a big liner for her day, 460 ft (140 m) long, 46 ft (14 m) wide and 35 ft (11 m) deep with a tonnage of 5400 tons (5500 t) gross. Her passenger capacity was 200 first class passengers, 130 second class and 300 steerage. A company announcement described the accommodation:

A great feature of the 1st class accommodation is the splendid saloon forward, free from the engine room, free from berths, running from side to side for 144 ft [44 m] and very lofty. It is fitted with electroplated brass furniture, carpeted and opening into the music saloon, where amid ferns and dracaenas, growing plentifully, a piano and organ are placed. The 3rd class accommodation supplies separate passages for £15. The chief saloon passengers have a promenade deck 160 ft [48 m] long and the whole breadth of the vessel for their exclusive use.

The *London Illustrated News* reported on her luxurious provisioning:

Cattle enough to stock a farm are carried to provide fresh meat and milk on the voyage out. A smaller ship of the Line takes out six bullocks, 100 sheep, 300 dozen of poultry and embarks twelve bullocks more at the Cape. Ice-rooms are fitted on the lower deck for carrying sixty tons of ice.

Chusan *and* Oriana

The change in the design and size of passenger steamers is dramatised by the contrast of these two ships.
The Chusan, built in 1852, was 190 ft (58 m) long and 29 ft (9 m) wide and had a top speed of 8 knots. She was the first steamer to carry mail to Australia and served Sydney, Melbourne, Singapore, Hong Kong and Calcutta before being sold to Japan in 1866. As an indication of the dangers faced by travellers in those days, the Chusan carried steam hoses to repel pirate attacks.
No such dangers faced the massive Oriana in her twenty-six years of service as a passenger liner and cruise ship. Built in 1960, she is 804 ft (245 m) long and 97 ft (30 m) wide. Like the Chusan, she was sold to the Japanese (in 1986) and is now a museum and entertainment piece in Beppo, Japan.

This was to change soon after when refrigeration was installed during her refit of 1881 and passenger capacity increased. Shortly after this electric lighting was fitted to all cabins making her the first ship on an Australian run with this feature.

The report on her engines is worthy of mention, however briefly: ". . . having 3 cylinders instead of the common 2, one high pressure 60 inches in diameter, the others low pressure 85 inches diameter, the propeller is 4 bladed and the boss of being of annealed cast iron and the blades of cast steel, diameter 22 ft., pitch 30 ft." Reversing was so simple, that "Lady Gertrude Boyle, on visiting the engine room during the experimental cruise on the Clyde, easily stopped and reversed the engines when going at their maximum speed, that is to say a young lady with one movement of her arm did what was tantamount to reining in 5,600 horses." Alas poor *Loch Ard*!

Steam was generated in four boilers each 15 ft 6 ins (4.5 m) diameter and with furnaces each 4 ft (1 m) diameter. Her stokers toiled and sweated to keep pressure to 75 pounds per square inch (517 kpa) for a steady speed of 16 knots. Their work was more than merely shovelling coal; valves and dials needed attention and bunkers large enough to hold sufficient coal for the voyage had to be trimmed.

SS *Orient*'s first voyage on 3 November 1879 established "the cool weather route" from Britain via the Cape with a full passenger list and the return with bunkers full of Australian coal along the shorter but hotter Suez Canal route, with fewer passengers but more Australian cargo. Later more effective ventilation was developed to beat the heat, engines became more reliable and sails were no longer considered necessary. All this and many other later innovations led to greater use of the canal and the epoch of the great liners of the twentieth century.

This extract from the Orient Line guidebook gives an inkling of what life on board *Orient* was like:

Gentlemen will do well to be provided with dressing suits which, with a cloak or overcoat, can be worn on deck in the early morning. When two or more are in the same cabin, it may save much inconvenience, as one or other can then postpone his dressing operations until the cabin is vacant. Ladies will find dressing-gowns and what are called "tea-gowns", very convenient in the tropics.

Every passenger should have a deckchair. It should be plainly marked with the owner's name in a conspicuous place, not on the back. A whole row of ladies may be disturbed because their names are on the backs of their chairs and someone is looking for his similarly-distinguished property. A chair that is not injured by being wet is the best. The common canvas deckchair is one of the worst, as it is not easily dried. Either a wooden seat, or wicker-work, or a canvas seat that can easily be removed and taken below should therefore be used.

She was built to Admiralty specifications for conversion to armed merchant cruiser or troop carrier, with watertight compartments and coal bunkers placed as protection for the engines. She trooped the guards to Alexandria when the Union Jack flew there in 1883, and in 1899 to 1902 she was on Boer War service, which included transport of Australian and New Zealand contingents.

Back in "civvies" in 1903 she resumed her regular mail, passenger and cargo services. In 1909, having completed sixty-six return voyages and having done her job well, she was sold to an Italian breakers' yard.

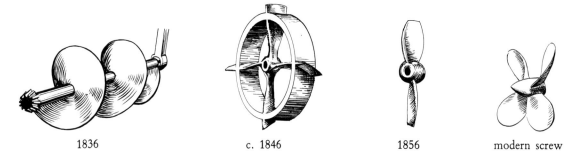

1836   c. 1846   1856   modern screw

The development of the screw propeller.

S S *Georgette*

FIRST SHIP IN THE WESTERN AUSTRALIAN NAVY

Western Australia, whose coastline was touched on by the early Dutchmen well before James Cook charted the New South Wales coastline, is Australia's largest state in area, but in 1870 it was the smallest in population. It did not lack, however, in thrusting enterprise, as the following extract from the *Inquirer and Commercial News* of 17 September 1873 testifies:

The example of a few men of energy may affect the welfare of a whole community, it may be the means of raising one of the largest territories of the globe from a state of apathy to that of activity and wealth. At last we are enabled to include in our budget the gratifying intelligence of regular steam communication along our coast.

The *News* was describing the arrival of a steamship from Britain a few days earlier.

The steamship was the *Georgette*. She had previously been advertised under the name *Western Australia* but someone, possibly a clerk in London, had omitted to change the registry and *Georgette* she remained. Her voyage out, with the captain's family as passengers, was via the by now accepted Suez Canal. It was unusual in that she made it completely under steam, although she was also rigged for sail.

Her intended purpose, to provide a regular service between Geraldton in the north and Albany in the south, calling in at Fremantle, Busselton and Bunbury, was achieved immediately and she proved highly successful. Her mail contracts with the Western Australian Government entailed timetabling of arrivals and departures to coincide with the movements of the new big mail liners from overseas. Business people and the local shopkeepers were pleased, and the community generally became accustomed to her appearance and to relying on her service.

The bare available statistics — 152 ft (46 m) long, 337 tons (342 t) gross, iron hull, single screw, compound engines, raised quarter deck, three anchors, two boats, engine-room skylights and other details — help to present a picture of a typical ship of her times, one of many engaged in the mundane but vital task of knitting our wide land together. But drama is never far away in the life of the humblest ship and for one exciting day she was the first ship in the Western Australian navy.

When the 1867 uprising in Ireland of the Fenian Brotherhood was suppressed the rebels were transported, and some were held in Fremantle gaol. The American branch of the brotherhood devised a bold plan to bring about a rescue. American whalers were frequent visitors to Western Australian waters and the most appropriate instrument for the rescue operation was a whaler.

At the time, the American whaling barque *Catalpa* was working off the coast and had put into Bunbury. Here the organiser of the escape contacted her captain who expressed his sympathy and agreed to assist in a well worked out plan.

Catalpa stood well out to sea, beyond the three-mile limit of territorial waters, leaving one of her boats on the beach just south of Fremantle. The telegraph line between Rockingham and Fremantle was cut and the convicts, some of whom were working on the roads, successfully completed their break. They made for the beach where the boat and their colleagues awaited, to row them out to *Catalpa*. They were almost there when the escape was discovered.

Georgette was lying in Fremantle harbour waiting to take on coal and cargo. She was ordered promptly by the Governor and Superintendent of Police to give chase. Heading out to *Catalpa*, she found that the escapees were not on board—they were still rowing out—and it was now dusk. There was nothing *Georgette* could do. The captain's quandary was soon resolved by the realisation that coal stocks were low. The only action *Georgette* could take was to return to Fremantle.

Hurriedly work gangs coaled her, while the local military mounted a twelve-pounder gun on her forecastle. Meanwhile the Fenians had climbed aboard *Catalpa*, which, owing to light wind overnight, had not moved very far. At dawn *Georgette* steamed out with police and gunners aboard to resume the chase, but *Catalpa* was now well out of territorial waters and the officials on *Georgette* had instructions to avoid an international incident. With a few Irish epithets to send them on the way, they returned to Fremantle and *Catalpa* sailed peacefully away. Her happy "bhoys" reached their Brothers in America. It was an incident for rejoicing in New York and is commemorated in folk song, one with an inevitable Irish lilt:

THE CATALPA

A noble whale ship and commander
Called the Catalpa, *they say,*
Came out to Western Australia
And took six poor Fenians away.

Seven long years had they served here
And seven long more had to stay,
For defending their country, old Ireland,
For that they were banished away.

You kept them in Western Australia
Till their hair began to turn grey,
When a Yank from the States of America
Came out here and stole them away.

Now all the Perth boats were a-racing,
And making short tacks for the spot;
But the Yankee she tacked into Fremantle,
And took the best prize of the lot.

The Georgette, armed with bold warriers,
Went out the poor Yanks to arrest,
But she hoisted her star-spangled banner,
Saying, "You'll not board me, I guess."

So remember those six Fenians colonial
And sing o'er these few verses with skill,
And remember the Yankees that stole them
And the home that they left on the hill.

Now they've landed safe in America
And there will be able to cry,
"Hoist up the green flag and shamrock,
Hurrah for old Ireland we'll die."

Chorus
So come all you screw warders and jailers,
Remember Perth regatta day,
Take care of the rest of your Fenians,
Or the Yankees will steal them away.

The painting depicts the scene at about 6 a.m. on 19 April 1876, as Georgette heads well out of Fremantle harbour towards Catalpa, *by now almost 32 kilometres out to sea.*

SS GEORGETTE

The columns of *The Times* in London reported the escapade at length and even included the first-hand reports of two of those involved—John Collins who organised the escape and James Wilson, one of the "felons". Sparing the British public no detail the "Thunderer" concluded:

It should be stated that when the men got off in the boat Collins fastened the following letter to a piece of wood and threw it on the water, believing that as the wind and tide were setting full on shore it would reach its destination:—

"To His Excellency the British Governor of Western Australia:—

"This is to certify that I have this day released from the clemency of Her Most Gracious Majesty Victoria, Queen of Great Britain, &c., six Irishmen condemned to imprisonment for life by the enlightened and magnanimous Government of Great Britain for having been guilty of the atrocious and unpardonable crimes known to the unenlightened portion of mankind as 'love of country' and 'hatred of tyranny'. For this act of 'Irish assurance,' my birth and blood being my full and sufficient warrant. Allow me to add that—

In taking my leave now, I've only to say,

"'A few cells I've emptied (a sell in its way);

"'I've the honour and pleasure to bid you good day—

"'From all future acquaintance excuse me, I pray.'"

It would have constituted an act of war had the Western Australian authorities taken a more vigorous action to apprehend the *Catalpa*, and memories of a court action against Britain for allowing the use of Melbourne during the American Civil War to the Confederate warship *Shenandoah* were fresh in their minds.

So *Georgette* returned to her workaday duties, her mail and cargo run and towing work. She was busily engaged thus until 1876. Then, while she was in Bunbury taking on 350 tons of cargo and seventy passengers for Albany, one of the heavy jarrah logs she was loading crashed into the hold. The damage was not noticed until she was well out to sea, when a serious leak developed and rapidly increased. Fires out and no steam to her engines, she sailed and drifted to the coast, grounding near Margaret River, a total loss.

SS *Adelaide*

THE MELBOURNE–ADELAIDE LINK

The term "liner" was by 1880 the accepted designation for a ship maintaining a regular service to a specified route; it later became identified particularly with passengers. By 1890 Australia's population exceeded three million, and included people of many nationalities. New arrivals first settled in the capital cities, which were not yet linked by railways or adequate roads.

Movement and trade between the states, already established by sail, was expanding and soon spread all around the coastline. As shipping lines reached out new "big" companies were formed. Competition for business intensified and was catered for by the steamship, which offered the regularity passengers sought.

SS *Adelaide* could be considered Australia's first passenger liner, as it was designed principally for passengers. She steamed into Port Adelaide on 6 January 1884 after a fifty-two-day run from her builders in Scotland. She came through the Suez Canal, which opened in 1869 and added to the advantages of steam, striking the final blow at sail which had been competitive on long voyages. An "open evening" was held aboard on 10 January—the arrival of a new ship was always a popular event. The proud people of Adelaide were excited by her appointments, especially by the innovation of electric lighting, then a novelty to most Australians.

The press was also profuse in its praises. The *Adelaide Observer* of 12 January reported in a lengthy welcome:

> *Top deck is taken up with skylights and companions, so necessary to ensuring light and ventilation to the dining rooms and staterooms. On entering the spacious vestibule, its space is centrally occupied by a broad flight of stairs, while around are lounges in most convenient positions.*

It went on to describe "the immense skylight fitted with choice plants, the piano amidship and a judicious arrangement of mirrors". There was praise for the polished timber panels, the gentlemen's smoking room and ladies' boudoir, the mosaic floor with the Australian coat of arms in the centre, the steam machine for making coffee and tea and the attention bestowed on the baths and lavatories and water closets, so well arranged as to ensure the comfort of passengers.

SS *Adelaide* used modern technology for 1883. Apart from electric lighting, she had a steam-powered steering system and a governor to control the engines when the ship pitched the propeller out of the water. The main mementoes of early days were the fore-and-aft sail-carrying masts but even these were of steel, as was the rigging used for derricks and cargo handling.

The company's directors and shareholders were also proud of their new ship. She was 279 ft (85 m) long, 33 ft (10 m) wide and 17 ft 6 ins (5.3 m) deep. Her tonnage was 1711 tons (1738 t) gross, and she accommodated 150 first class passengers in cabins situated amidships and 152 second class passengers in cabins situated abaft the funnel. She also had space for 1000 tons (1016 t) of general cargo.

SS *ADELAIDE*

Adelaide averaged 14 knots on the Melbourne–Adelaide run and acquired the title of the fastest steamer in Australia. This led to her only mishap. It was a frequent practice when meeting a rival to challenge for a race. When her rival for the title, *Wiarapara*, left the Yarra River at the same time in February 1884, the race was on to the heads of Port Phillip, and they collided in the narrow West Channel. It was only a glancing blow and *Adelaide* continued with her voyage. Both skippers were reprimanded, but one of the rules of the sea had been broken and *Adelaide*'s skipper was suspended for two months.

In 1886 her regular run included Sydney. In 1894 she was serving the demands of the West Australian goldrush, running to Fremantle and Albany. Then in 1895 she opened the service from Melbourne to Townsville in north Queensland, in which she served until succeeded by the new, larger and faster ships at the turn of the century.

The change from sail to steam during mid-century was gradual and slow, but once steam was firmly established changes came quickly. *Adelaide* could not compete in the growing passenger trade along the coast and she was put up for sale.

In 1906 she was bought by Birt and Company of Sydney and was fitted with refrigeration machinery. She was then sold to Elvanger Brothers of Vladivostok and served as a store ship. This was the beginning of a long period of many changes which continued with the Kousnetsoff Brothers of Vladivostok taking over ownership in 1911 and in 1912 selling her to a Mr W. Katz of Shanghai. Another ownership change in 1913 to Goshi Kishimoto Shoki of Japan brought a name change as well and she became *Shinten Maru*.

Then in 1915 Moller and Company of Shanghai acquired her for service along the China coast and renamed her *Castleford*. This was the name of a racehorse owned by one of the Moller brothers who, it is believed, won the ship in a racecourse bet. In 1919 she had yet another name change to become *Ralph Moller* and, after a refit and new boilers, she spent a further four years in Moller's service. She was then sold to Lien Wen Wei of Shanghai and renamed *Hofung* and later, when the South China Steamship Company became her new owner, she was renamed yet again to *Hwah Yang*.

In 1930 *Adelaide/Hwah Yang* changed owners for the tenth time—her last change. Her long eventful life was ended in 1931 when she was wrecked in the East China Sea.

In her day she had been a crack liner. She was small by the standards of the liners of later years but she heralded a new style of coastal sea travel, and to Australians she was always affectionately remembered as "the good old *Adelaide*"—the ship that pioneered new standards of passenger comfort.

With the majestic bearing of a true liner, Adelaide *is shown here in her early pride, pushing her sharp straight stem through a lively sea and a fresh wind.*

SS *Strathleven*

FRESH MEAT TO BRITAIN

Australian poets and songwriters, and more recently our film-makers, have romanticised the cattleman and his mates from the bush. But it was on the unsung, quiet achievement of one shipping enterprise, one voyage and one ship that the stage was set for their fame, and that the meat industry climbed to importance. The ship was SS *Strathleven*, the voyage Melbourne to London, 6 December 1879.

It was an event widely appreciated in the London newspapers. *The Times* for 9 February 1888 reported:

A number of persons interested in the colonies and in shipping of this country, were invited to East India docks on Friday to judge for themselves the degree of success which attended the experiment in the importation of fresh meat from Australia by Messrs. McIlwraith McEacharn and Company.

It went on to describe profusely the construction of the freezing chamber to hold 30 tons of meat and to recount how lunch was served on board:

all the principal dishes consisting of fresh meat may be said to have shown that beef and mutton of very good quality can be obtained in Australia and can be landed in England unaffected by the voyage in such condition that neither by its appearance in the butcher shop, nor by any peculiarities of flavour when cooked for the table could it be distinguished from freshly killed English meat. It was stated that meat could be produced in Australia and sold in quantity there at the profit of less than 2 pence per pound and that probably 2 pence would cover the cost of bringing it over.

A few days later "Letters to the Editor" contained a note of further significance:

The interesting fact in the "The Times" of Monday, of the first successful importation of fresh meat from Australia is worthy of far more attention than has been given to it. The accomplishment of this achievement has been looked forward to for many years with great interest by the Queen's subjects in the Southern Colonies. From the superfluity they have hoped that some day they might supply the necessities of the old country. The late Mr. Mort of Sydney, it is said, spent £70,000 from his private fortune, in work and experiment for preserving meat in fresh condition by freezing.

The letter described meat stocks in Australia and explained how this invention affected Australian cattlemen and the vast population in England.

A carcase of lamb was sent to Queen Victoria at Buckingham Palace and a sheep to the Prince of Wales. The

SS Strathleven is shown in Australian waters in pleasant conditions allowing her to set her fore and aft sails to save coal and steady her roll. She is in the serviceable, utilitarian colours of black hull and funnel.

SS *STRATHLEVEN*

Travellers Club, London, received a joint of beef and when Lord Hatherton lunched at the club he is reported to have remarked on the fine quality of the meat and expressed some surprise that it had come all the way from Australia. Further, he feared that this new import trade from the colony may be a hidden threat to the industry of his own tenant farmers.

The British press was enthusiastic and the traders of the famous Smithfield Market in London had every reason to be more so. The meat had cost 1½ to 2 pence per pound and was sold at 4¼ to 5 pence per pound for the beef and 5¼ to 6 pence per pound for mutton. Australia's potential as a source of meat was thus brought to the attention of the British population.

The voyage of the *Strathleven* followed an inquiry held by a group of Queensland squatters into a shipment of meat from Argentina to France in 1878. Andrew McIlwraith, who was in London at the time, investigated the story and inspected the ship but reported that a different freezing method would be required for the longer voyage through the tropics from Australia. No time was lost. Messrs Bell and Coleman, Engineers of Glasgow designed a freezing plant suitable for these conditions. SS *Strathleven*, a tramp steamer awaiting cargo, was chartered, the freezing machinery installed, and in 1879 she sailed from Britain on her epoch-making voyage. She sailed from Sydney in November 1879, called in at Melbourne and was back in the East India Docks, London, on 2 February 1880 with 40 tons of butter, beef, lamb and mutton in prime condition. A syndicate of businessmen, producers and agencies was involved but the risk of the venture was borne by McIlwraith McEacharn, which became one of Australia's leading shipping companies.

Strathleven is described in Lloyds' register 1878:

1588 tons [1613 t] nett, 2436 tons [2474 t] gross, 2257 tons [2293 t] under deck, 320 ft. 9 ins. [98 m] long, 36 ft. [11 m] broad, 26 ft. [8 m] deep. Iron hull and decks, 3 decks laid. Engines, compound inverted 2 cylinder, 38 ins., 70 ins., boiler pressure 70 pound per square inch, 220 h.p., built by Blackwood and Gordon, Glasgow 1875. Owner Burrell & Sons, Glasgow.

These cold, bare statistics convey nothing of the importance of her voyage or of its effect on Australia's meat and dairy industries. This was *Strathleven*'s one and only visit to Australia. After that historic voyage her refrigeration machinery was removed and she continued a useful working life as a general cargo carrier. This period of her career was almost unrecorded until she foundered in an Atlantic gale in 1901 while on a passage to Mexico.

She was just a tramp steamer, one of the many that constituted more than ninety per cent of Britain's Merchant Navy and which, at that time, were spreading British influence via the sea lanes of the world. A tramp ship was a cargo carrying vessel without a regular route. It could be sent to a port to pick up cargo for delivery to any other port. When no cargo was available the tramp would go "light", in ballast, to wherever a cargo awaited shipment. She could be away for long periods and her seamen often did not see their families for over a year.

Britain's poets—Kipling, Newbolt, Masefield and others—have eulogised these humble ships and seamen. It was Kipling who wrote the following with the tramp ship in mind:

And where will you fetch it from, all you big steamers,
And where shall I write you when you are away?
We fetch it from Melbourne, Quebec and Vancouver,
Address us at Hobart, Hong Kong and Bombay

SS *Guthrie*

BURNS PHILP BEGINNINGS

The story of the famous Burns Philp Company starts in a manner similar to those of many other early companies in Australia—with one man. He was Jimmy Burns, born Edinburgh 1846, a young immigrant cum businessman.

He arrived in Brisbane in 1862 aged sixteen and was soon employed as a shopkeeper in various Queensland towns near the new goldfields. In 1870 the death of his father drew him back to Scotland. However, after three years, with his carefully accumulated savings supplemented by funds from his father's estate, he returned and opened a store at Cleveland Bay, Townsville, then a thriving centre. At that time ship owning was far from James Burns' mind, although as a native of what was then the busiest shipbuilding country in the world, he must have had some interest in ships.

Quite early in his Townsville days, to meet competition from his rivals, he was compelled to charter a ship to bring supplies from Sydney. By 1874 he was officially a shipowner. He already had a few anonymous small craft, such as lighters, for unloading the larger ships that called at the coastal towns of north Queensland where he owned stores. His first registered vessel was a little cutter named *Henry Albert*, then he acquired a large ketch of 51 tons (52 t), *Dawn*. Steamers were soon added to his growing fleet as well as smart brigantines such as *Ivanhoe* which traded beyond the coastal towns of north Queensland. They voyaged eastwards to the Pacific Islands, south to Sydney and around the "Top End" to Darwin and the Gulf ports. His other commercial interests reached inland to Charters Towers. James Burns' business prospered and he grew into a fellow of considerable substance.

The tropical malarial mosquito, however, respects nobody. Badly affected by malaria, Burns moved to Sydney in 1887 on medical advice, but his Queensland interests were not abandoned. He formed a partnership with a local merchant, Robert Philp, and the new company expanded to ownership of a large fleet of passenger and cargo liners, trading to Japan, Hong Kong and other eastern ports.

To meet the growing traffic, Burns Philp Company bought two steamers in 1904 from one of their competitors in the service. These were *Airlie* and *Guthrie*, built in 1884 for the Eastern and Australian Steamship Company by Doxfords of Sunderland. These elegant sisters with graceful lines, clipper-bowed and figurehead ornamented, formed a particularly distinctive pair; the only visible difference between the two was in the rigging.

They were 314 ft (96 m) long and 38 ft (12 m) wide and each was powered by a compound engine with cylinders 40 inches and 73 inches in diameter and two double-ended boilers. A speed of 14 knots was attainable; 12 knots was service speed. Tasteful accommodation of thirty-six first class passengers was located around the saloon, which according to newspapers of the day was "replete with every convenience".

A punkah fan system provided the extra ventilation needed for comfort in the tropics. Wash basins, which when not in use were folded back against the bulkheads (cabin walls), were fitted in all cabins. Twenty-four second class passengers were also comfortably accommodated, as well as an unrecorded but large number in steerage.

SS GUTHRIE

Island Traders

⚓ *The brigantine* Ivanhoe *was one of a number of small sailing vessels used by the Burns Philp Company in the 1890s to trade with Normanton, Cairns and other north Queensland ports and the Pacific Islands. The trading consisted of general cargo for the islands' stores, as well as labour for the sugarfields of Queensland and island produce such as coconuts for the Australian market.*

Guthrie came out first, leaving Britain in May 1884 in time to reach Hong Kong and Foochow for the new season's tea for Australia. She arrived in Sydney on 28 August 1884 via Darwin and Queensland ports. *Airlie* followed two months later. The sisters rendered good service to the Eastern and Australian Steamship Company for twenty years. In 1904 when they changed dress to wear the Burns Philp flag with the thistle emblem and the black and white chequered funnel, more ports were added to their itinerary: Thursday Island, New Guinea, Singapore, as well as an occasional call into Derby, Western Australia, to feed the miners and other new settlers on the north-west coast.

⚓ *With the background of Townsville's Castle Peak,* Guthrie *is shown steaming out to sea across the sheltered waters of Cleveland Bay.*

107

In 1905, to meet the demand for frozen meat in Singapore, both ships were fitted with refrigeration space for 300 tons (305 t) of meat. The installation was designed and built in Australia, and Australian beef and mutton always arrived in perfect condition. On one of her voyages *Guthrie* took 300 tons of Australian coal for hulking in Singapore, in addition to a full quota of meat and other produce of Australia.

As trading from Australia increased, Surabaya, Semarang and Batavia (Jakarta) were included in the service. The sisters had their share of tropical typhoons and survived minor accidents, inevitable in a sea career, but generally they enjoyed a fairly uneventful and successful span of service.

In 1912, when more modern ships were added to the fleet, the sisters were sold to China for service based on Hong Kong and Malaya. They were among the early leaders in a period that marked a new outward-looking, enterprising Australia and confirmed a new mature status of our country in the Pacific area.

ss *Casino*

THE BELFAST AND KOROIT STEAM NAVIGATION COMPANY

Just as the early pastoralists and merchants of New South Wales had combined new business interests to form shipping companies, incidentally stimulating the general growth of the area, so did others of their enterprising kind do the same in the later developments of new areas around the coastline of Australia.

In Victoria, the gentlemen of the flourishing Western District formed the Belfast and Koroit Steam Navigation Company and were seeking a suitable ship for service between Portland, Port Fairy, Warrnambool, Apollo Bay and Melbourne.

By a lucky coincidence a little steamer called into Warrnambool to replenish her coal bunkers on 30 May 1882. It was the SS *Casino*, which had left her builders' yard in Scotland on 18 March 1882 on a delivery voyage to join the northern New South Wales coastal service. A visitor to an isolated community, as Warrnambool then was, was always a great event. For Victoria it was also a fortunate one.

The directors of the new company inspected her and, being favourably impressed, bought her immediately and *Casino*, named for a town in northern New South Wales, remained in Victoria. Rigged as a three-masted schooner, she carried sail to economise on coal on the long voyage out. But sail was less important on the short coastal trips and so later her mainmast was removed and accommodation was increased.

She was registered at Port Fairy (Shire of Belfast) and commenced her new service on 29 July 1882. A successful, if eventful, career of fifty years followed.

Casino's successes were a result of her fitness for purpose. Her tonnage was 425 tons (432 t) gross; she was 160 ft (49 m) long and 24 ft (7 m) wide, and fully laden she drew 10 ft (3 m), not too small to handle the seas, not too big to handle the poor harbour conditions. Her inverted compound engines turned a single screw, giving a service speed of 10 knots which could be pushed to 12 knots. She had good accommodation for seventy-one passengers. Her saloon, located amidships away from the noise and smells of engines, was lofty compared with those of other ships of her size, and there was more accommodation in the fore cabin. Portland to Melbourne fares were advertised at ten shillings single, fifteen shillings return in the saloon, five shillings single and seven shillings and sixpence return in steerage.

By the 1920s she was practically the only trader on the route carrying passengers. Ship/train tickets on the new railway line to Melbourne were available.

Casino was equally useful as a cargo carrier. She had hold space for 300 tons (305 t) of mixed cargo which varied with the seasons. It cost only five shillings to send a ton of potatoes to Melbourne from Warrnambool in the potato season. Her hold and deck space could take the long timbers being used for the piers and jetties then growing out from the beaches to form new "harbours". In short, as the local newspapers put it, she was "ideal for the west coast service".

SS CASINO

Victoria's south-west coast is not ideal for ships: it is studded with wreck sites and it is a rich field for modern marine archaeologists. What were then designated harbours were little more than long exposed jetties reaching out through the breaking surf to deeper unprotected waters facing Bass Strait. Many reefs and sandbanks were discovered at great cost by the early seamen under sail and steam and more than good seamanship was necessary for survival. *Casino* grounded on her very first voyage but was undamaged. She often touched bottom in the troughs of big waves while entering or leaving harbour. This was taken as normal, a mere occupational hazard, in these coastal waters.

In 1924 *Casino* struck an unmarked reef near Point Howden and most of her cargo was off-loaded before she refloated. What came ashore was mainly Christmas cheer destined for the citizens of Portland and Warrnambool, but workers on the Great Ocean Road, then under construction, were the chief beneficiaries. *Casino* limped back to Melbourne for repairs. Again in 1929 she struck a rock when entering Lady Bay, Warrnambool, at night—it was a poorly marked entrance with only one navigation mark. Back to Melbourne she went again for repairs to a damaged hull.

She survived many such incidents and despite all this, patronage of her continued. In January 1932, the Melbourne *Argus* predicted that "her future seems assured with many more years ahead". It was in this her fiftieth year that her owners decided to refit and repaint her as a birthday celebration.

SS *Casino* left Melbourne on 9 July 1932 with a cargo of 240 tons (244 t), mostly sugar. The next day was blowing a hard southerly, and as she was approaching the long jetty at Apollo Bay her anchor was dropped to assist in the manoeuvre of coming alongside, but this time the normal procedure proved fatal. She surged in the big sea, bumped the shallow bottom and tore her hull on her anchor. Badly holed and down by the head, with her engine-room flooding, she rolled over and sank. Ten seamen were lost; her passengers and seven crew members made it safely to the shore.

Casino's binnacle, steering wheel, anchor and other salvage are her memorial, displayed in the ports she served for a record period on that route.

Casino *is seen here under a leaden winter sky steaming through the icy waters of Bass Strait.*

SS *Edina*

THE LUCKY EXCURSIONIST

Luck and a long and exciting life followed the launching of *Edina* at Barclay Curle shipyard in Glasgow in 1854. Her statistics were unimpressive; she was a modest little ship 171 ft (52 m) long, 23 ft (7 m) wide and 12 ft 7 ins (4 m) deep, 322 tons (327 t) gross. She was a single-screw iron steamer but, as with all steamships built during this early period of sail-to-steam transition, her engines were considered as auxiliary to her sails and she was schooner-rigged.

Her working life began with trading from Hull to Hamburg across the North Sea, but after a short period of peaceful work she was diverted to carrying supplies to the Black Sea, for the forces fighting in the Crimean War. Horses and military stores and materials constituted her main cargoes, as well as some equipment for Florence Nightingale's hospital at Scutari. After that war she resumed her former peacetime trade for some years.

1863 saw her as a blockade runner during the American Civil War. She plied the Atlantic and brought cotton from Galveston, Texas, to the mills of Manchester, Lancashire. For this traffic a third sail-carrying mast was added and it was in this rig that she came to Australia in 1864. Travelling via the Cape and under sail all the way, she reached Melbourne in just 104 days after leaving Glasgow.

Edina became an Australian vessel in 1864 when she was bought by Stephen Henty of the famous Portland family, and served the growing trade between Portland, Warrnambool and Melbourne, her new port of registry. *Edina* made several trips taking diggers to New Zealand during the Otago gold rush in 1861 and there were several trips when she visited Tasmanian ports. Wherever she was, she always seemed to be in the public eye. When the Duke of Edinburgh visited Melbourne in 1867, she was conspicuously positioned in the escort of ships steaming up Port Phillip Bay.

In 1875 she was sold to the Howard Smith Steamship Company, who altered her for passenger service along the Queensland coast. This lasted for five successful years after which she returned to Melbourne and took on the run to Portarlington and Geelong. However, even this comparatively sheltered 160 kilometre return voyage from her berth in the Yarra River was not devoid of newsmaking events.

The most serious of these of these were collisions in what was then a very busy waterway, especially at the entrance to the Yarra River. It was near this area in 1898 that she collided with the steamer *Manuwatu*. *Edina* went on to the beach near Williamstown but, undamaged, floated off and resumed her voyage on the next tide; *Manuwatu* sank. In July of the next year, winter and a time of morning fog in Port Phillip Bay, *Edina* ran into the steamer

In excursion bunting Edina *is shown moving through the fleets of small gaff-rigged yachts typical of the 1920–30 period.*

SS *EDINA*

Excelsior. No lives were lost but had it not been for *Edina*'s fiddle bow, it could have been a tragedy. A straight vertical knife-like steamer stem which was becoming common at that time would have inflicted greater damage. However, the gentle curve acted as a cushion. *Excelsior* sank but all passengers and crew climbed aboard *Edina* and she returned to Melbourne only slightly damaged.

Edina's luck held in a number of such incidents, most of them in the same area, the narrow mouth of the Yarra. She ran aground occasionally, she sank a tug and a barge, but she always came off best. Hers seemed to be a charmed life.

In May 1917 she was refitted with new boilers and cabin structure, which further improved passenger accommodation. Her run to Geelong became a popular Saturday afternoon excursion. Less serious incidents in *Edina*'s career occurred during this part of her service. There was, for example, the over-merry excursionist who walked overboard as *Edina* was steaming upriver to her berth—he thought he was nearing home!

In her eighty-fourth year, 1938, despite public protest, she was taken out of service, stripped down to a coal hulk and rechristened *Dinah*. She was totally scrapped in 1958.

"Old *Edina*" seems to have been a popular discussion topic in the Flinders Street hotels in Melbourne. In Geelong her popularity is commemorated by a special room in the City Hall.

HMAS *Sydney*

AUSTRALIA GOES TO WAR

Australians are reputedly a friendly, easygoing people, not given to militaristic jingoism, but they are certainly, if quietly, quite proud of Australia's growth to nationhood which many consider came to maturity through military action—the Gallipoli landing during the Great War 1914–18.

The Royal Australian Navy provided some of the first Australians with an opportunity to go into action at the outbreak of hostilities. These were members of a special naval Military Expeditionary Force which seized German New Guinea and destroyed several German radio stations in the Pacific. The light cruiser HMAS *Sydney* was part of that action, its first real blooding coming not long after.

HMAS Sydney II

This cruiser, the second Australian warship to bear the name Sydney, *saw successful action in the Mediterranean during World War II, where she sank the Italian cruiser,* Bartolomeo Colleoni, *in March 1941. In November of that year, while on escort duty in the Indian Ocean, she engaged the German raider* Kormoran. *Both ships were sunk, and of Sydney's crew of 645 not one survived.*

HMAS *SYDNEY*

On 1 November 1914 a convoy of forty-two ships carrying the 1st, 2nd and 3rd Australian divisions and a division of New Zealand troops—15 000 troops in all—left Albany, Western Australia, for the Middle East. Escorts were a British cruiser, two Australian light cruisers and a Japanese battle cruiser.

At 6.40 a.m. on 9 November, when the convoy was about 95 kilometres from the Cocos Islands, a radio message was received from the islands' transmitter: "Three funnelled warship off island, landing a party in boats." The German raider SMS *Emden* was suspected. By 7.00 HMAS *Sydney* was racing away from the convoy towards her first real action. Meanwhile the German landing party had demolished the islands' radio installation, but they were not yet back on board their ship when they sighted *Sydney*'s smoke. *Emden* was identified; shorthanded, the ship weighed anchor, steamed out of harbour and cleared for battle. On board *Sydney* they had identified *Emden* and battle stations were sounded.

Action opened at 9.40 but the fighting was swiftly over. *Emden*, built in 1906, had been at sea for four months and had sunk twenty-three merchant ships in her brief commerce-raiding cruise. *Sydney* was fresh and itching for a scrap. At 10.45 *Emden*'s guns ceased firing and she headed on to a reef on North Keeling Island, where she came to rest a battered charnel-house. One hundred and thirty-four of her sailors were killed, more were wounded; Sydney lost four men and had twelve wounded.

After attending to wounded and observing the conventions of war, *Sydney* rejoined the convoy at Colombo. Then it was on to Malta for refit and refuel. Freshened up again, she proceeded to new duties in the Atlantic, where the U-boat menace was increasing. Her task included patrols with HMAS *Melbourne* from the Caribbean northwards to Canada along the eastern seaboard of America to prevent German shipping from finding sanctuary possible at that time as the USA was a neutral country.

Then, in September 1916 came a new, more intense period of action. *Sydney*, together with *Melbourne*, was sent to the grim North Sea which was liberally provisioned with mines, U-boats and bomb laden aircraft. Here she joined the Second Light Cruiser Squadron whose main activities were in support of destroyers and minesweepers. She had been properly refitted for this role, but nothing had prepared her for her most terrifying enemy—the North Sea itself. To sailors accustomed to the blue waters of Australia, the Indian Ocean, the Mediterranean and the Caribbean, these inhospitable waters came as a violent shock. Cold heavy seas swept her decks, smashing life-boats and breaking or bruising many a limb.

It was on 4 May 1917 while on North Sea patrol that *Sydney* was attacked by a German zeppelin which tried to bomb her. The zeppelin stayed high and out of range of *Sydney*'s gunners but fortunately it was also too high for any accuracy with bombs and nobody was hurt.

During another refit at Chatham in 1917 the port was heavily bombed and many sailors were killed in barracks. *Sydney* left the Chatham dockyard wearing a new, more pugnacious face—her elegant tall single-pole mast had been replaced by a heavy tripod mast, bearing a new fire-control top and her bridge protection was strengthened.

Modifications at Chatham also equipped her with a revolving aeroplane launching platform forward of the

HMAS Sydney *is shown on a nice day in the North Sea, a more appropriate and worklike setting than the blue sunlit seas of Australia.*

bridge and a Sopwith aircraft to go with it. This was one of the very early experiments with naval aircraft and was put to the test in battle months later when *Sydney* and *Melbourne* both launched their fighters to chase two German reconnaissance aircraft in Heligoland Bight. *Sydney*'s fighter attacked and probably destroyed one of the enemy machines.

Her statistics included: protective armour-plating 3 ins (7.5 cm) thick on the sides and 2 ins (5 cm) thick on the deck; displacement tonnage 5400 (5486 t), length 457 ft (139 m), beam 50 ft (15 m), draught 18 ft (5.5 m). Her four screws were driven by Parson's turbines and gave her a speed of 25½ knots at a cruising range of 4000 miles (6400 km). She had eight six-inch guns, one anti-aircraft gun and two 21 inch torpedo tubes, as well as minor light weapons. She had a total complement of 390.

She returned home after four years of continuous active service. In 1920 she was taken off the active fleet list but put to service for "show the flag" cruises, Australia Day regattas and similar pleasant duties. In 1929 she was broken up at Cockatoo dockyard in Sydney. Her tripod mast now stands at Bradley's Head in Sydney Harbour and a section of her bow is mounted in the harbourside wall at Kirribilli. These souvenirs serve to commemorate a great ship and her part in Australia's entry on to the world stage.

The 18 Footers

UNIQUELY MADE IN AUSTRALIA

Sydney Harbour, Saturday afternoon, about 150 years after the First Fleeters landed — could those sad souls have imagined such a scene?

The sailing ship founded Australia. It was therefore inevitable that the bravura of billowing canvas would have been absorbed into a lusty new lifestyle. It was also inevitable that a fresh spirit of egalitarianism would flourish, as the oppressive cloud of convict years and military government were replaced by free settlers living in a free country.

The unfenced sea and the free wind made yachting, once considered the preserve of the wealthy leisured gentlemen of the Georgian and Victorian eras, more easily accessible to all. Australia's first races were between boat

Eighteen Footers

Mele Bilo *of Western Australia and* Britannia *of New South Wales were famous eighteen footers of the 1920s and 1930s.* Mele Bilo, *Australian National Champion of 1921, is pictured running free off the wind.* Britannia, *with the Red Ensign emblazoned on her mainsail, is crossing astern on a close reach.*

Eighteen Footers

crews of visiting vessels but it was not long before prosperous waterfront merchants, shopkeepers and tradesmen clubbed together to organise races. As early as 1858 a little cutter with revolutionary keel and section took to the water from Woolloomooloo Bay. She was called *Australian*.

Soon miners from the suburb of Balmain, butchers, bakers, everybody and anybody was "having a go". Boat building boomed along the waterfront. In 1891 the Sydney Flying Squadron was founded and a unique, characteristically Australian design developed. An open type boat, easy to launch from the beach and with unceremonious informality typical of Australians, it became known simply as the Eighteen Footer, which was its length.

Five years later these unmistakable craft were reported as "typical" by a visiting American, Joshua Slocum:

> *The typical Sydney boat is a handy sloop of great beam and enormous sail-carrying power; but a capsize is not uncommon, for they carry sail like Vikings. In Sydney I saw all manner of craft, from the smart steam launch and sailing-cutter to the smaller sloop and canoe pleasuring the bay. Everybody owned a boat. If a boy in Australia has not the means to buy him a boat, he builds one, and it is usually not one to be ashamed of.*

The Eighteen Footer was eight feet (2.4 m) wide and undecked, with straight stem and broad transom stern, a shallow section, and a deep dagger-shaped centreboard. Its sail area was enormous. The mainsail reached from a high-peaked gaff out over the stern on a 30 ft (9 m) boom, and a 20 ft (6 m) bowsprit led the foresail ahead. When running, the huge spinnaker ballooned out from the main peak to a 45 ft (14 m) pole and there were many extras. In the "pile on the canvas" tradition of the old clipper ships, many extra sails could be added to this large area—ballooner, ringtail, topsail, watersail or any windcatching contraption the skipper could invent.

It was a tough sport, with canvas sails that hardened when wet, Manila ropes that tore the skin, no winches to ease muscle strain, heavy blocks and many bruised knuckles. Masochistic maybe, but lots of fun.

The racing was close-matched and, despite the rugged individualism of the skippers and crews, differences between the boats were minor and rare; it was often only the sail marking that distinguished one boat from another. Competition was keen and the atmosphere and excitement of the scene was intense. Betting took place on board the spectator-packed steam ferries and launches that crowded into the picture and the sports journalists recorded the spectacle for an even wider audience to appreciate:

> *The westerly squall which swept the Harbour on Saturday afternoon wrought havoc among competitors in the Sydney (Sailing) Club's race. In many instances, skippers were caught napping, and they, together with their respective crews, were speedily in the water. Other competitors were disabled to such an extent that they could not continue the contest—while several wisely lowered away until the squall—which only lasted a few minutes—abated. Though very trying for the competitors, the sport was full of exciting situations, the onlooking public being kept at a high pitch whilst the sensational incidents lasted. So boisterous were the conditions that the pilot boat Captain Cook steamed out of Watsons Bay and proceeded to the distressed boats, while the water police, in their launch, had a particularly busy time picking up crews, etc.*
> Sydney Morning Herald, 1914

⚓ *The two boats shown here are unidentified. They are pictured on Sydney Harbour sailing "off the wind", spinnakers flying, crew piling out to windward, bailer boy hidden in the shadow of the bulging mainsail.*

By the turn of the century the eighteen footer flourished and clubs were established Australia-wide. They were racing in 1905 in Brisbane and 1907 in Perth, and National Championships were held in these states regularly. Titles were fairly evenly distributed. By 1930 it became a more tightly organised sport; more refinements and limitations in design were introduced and speeds of more than 20 knots were reached during wind bursts.

The eighteen footer of today has developed on aerodynamic lines towards a factory-built lighter hull, rigged with modern lightweight materials and balanced by a small crew of three or four athletic men swinging out on a trapeze. More costly than the old time "handmade" timber job, the new lady is commercially sponsored and is faster still. A speed of 20 knots or more is quite commonplace when the wind blows. Where the old-timers drove heavily through the seas, the new boats skim and skip like a seabird across the surface. The spirit of the sailors is still the same.

In recent years the popularity of sailing has increased and the number of types of yachts has multiplied; our harbour scene is crowded with bright sails. But Sydney's Eighteen Footer Race is still the most spectacular of the weekly racing events and still attracts the largest "Sat'dee arvo" audience.

T S S *Taroona*

BASS STRAIT STEAMER

By 1890 all except one of our coastal capital cities were linked by railways; it was 1917 before Perth joined the network. Popularity came slowly to long-distance railway travel; it was either too hot and dusty or too cold and bumpy, and changes of railway gauge at state borders contributed to the discomfort. Passenger travel by sea had become a good habit and continued well into the 1930s. Many fine steamers such as *Kanimbla* and *Manoora* had established a uniquely Australian tradition, stemming from the ability to turn a voyage into a social event. On shipboard there was time to relax and be friendly with fellow travellers and to find relief from the dry land.

The tradition still persists. The Bass Strait ferry still operates regularly between Melbourne and the "Island State", Tasmania. The service is maintained at present by a modern new ship named to commemorate the Dutch

Manoora

Manoora *was the last liner on the Australian coast, serving the Adelaide Steamship Company from 1935 to 1961, when she was sold to the Indonesian Government. Like all good ships of her time, she was commandeered for war service in 1939 and was converted first to armed merchant cruiser and later to infantry landing ship serving in the Milne Bay, Lingayen Gulf, Tarakan and other actions. She was 450 ft (138 m) long and 65 ft (20 m) wide and is depicted here in war paint, showing the fashionable cruiser stern.*

Kanimbla

Kanimbla *was a 490 ft (150 m) by 66 ft (20 m) liner built in 1936 for McIlwraith McEacharn's Australian coastal service. During World War II she saw service as an armed merchant cruiser, and from 1943 as an infantry landing ship participating in the Pacific Islands campaign. Refitted in 1949, she resumed service on the coast until sold in 1961 to Indonesia. With a new name,* Oriental Queen, *she began yet another career, this time carrying Moslem pilgrims to the Middle East. She finally met her end in a breaker's yard in 1975.*

TSS TAROONA

navigator Abel Tasman. Before her came a long list of smart ships very popular in their days. *Taroona* was one of these.

The *Launceston Examiner* in October 1936 reported:

A regular steamer service for passengers and cargo is provided between Launceston and Melbourne and Burnie and Devonport and Melbourne by five sailings weekly. These sailings are maintained by the new luxurious T.S.S. Taroona and the T.S.S. Nairana. The journey by either steamer does not occupy more than 17 hours, is mostly at night and includes 72 miles [115 km] of sheltered waters at both ends of the journey in Port Phillip Bay, Melbourne and 40 miles [64 km] of the beautiful Tamar River, Launceston. The Taroona is a new luxury miniature liner of 4,286 tons [4355 t] especially built on modern lines for the Tasmanian–Melbourne service. It has all the latest equipment for handling cargo and is designed to give maximum comfort to passengers when at sea. Its appointments and service are of the highest standard and provide accommodation of every kind.

Taroona was built in Glasgow in 1935 for Tasmanian Steamers Ltd, a company formed after the merger of Huddart Parker Co. and Union Steamship Co. The hull and funnel colours represent this combination. She was a model of the big liners of the period, with the then fashionable cruiser stern and she was the pride of Tasmania.

She measured 338 ft (103 m) long, 50 ft (15 m) wide and 24 ft (7.5 m) deep, and had accommodation for 483 passengers with a crew of eighty-five, plus stowage for thirty motor cars and refrigerated cargo space. Her oil-fired boilers pushed steam into six turbine engines geared to two screws which gave her a speed of 18 knots. At this speed she maintained a tightly regular service of three trips weekly, over 2500 kilometres, a schedule only rarely broken by minor accidents which are part of the life of any hard-worked ship.

But one dramatic event disturbed her routine. In May 1936 she was badly damaged by fire while at her wharf in the Yarra. After a two months' refit she was back on the job, in conjunction with *Nairana* providing five return sailings weekly across Bass Strait.

This continued until she was called up for war service. Her first task was to take New Zealand troops to Suva in March 1942. In the RAN as a fast troop carrier she seemed to have been blessed with a charmed life. On two occasions while stuck fast aground near Port Moresby, New Guinea, she was a sitting target for Japanese bombers, but she escaped unscathed.

On both occasions *Taroona* freed herself, refuelled in Port Moresby and returned to Townsville to continue a trouble-free troop shuttle service between Australia's northern ports and various island theatres of war. Her good luck held throughout ninety-four trips, totalling 330 000 kilometres of steaming, often in the firing line. Her war service terminated in February 1946 after her arrival in Sydney with 644 happy homecoming service personnel.

She returned to "civvies" on Bass Strait in 1946 after an extensive overhaul which included a change in contours. Her two short funnels were replaced by a single taller one, a change in appearance which did not seem to please the shiplovers of Tasmania. Her service continued in the face of growing competition from the airlines until as a twenty-five year old lady she was sold to Tynaldos Brothers of Athens in 1959.

Henty and Batman would have sailed the same wide stretch of the sheltered Tamar River in which Taroona *is depicted. The small clinker-built sailing boat moored in the foreground is a typical timber craft of the times.*

Manunda

Manunda *was a coastal passenger liner owned by the Adelaide Steamship Company and was especially popular with Australian racegoers, being always booked for trips to Melbourne for "The Cup". After ten successful years on the coast, she was called up for war service in 1939 and converted to a hospital ship. Heavily damaged during the 1943 bombing of Darwin, she was quickly repaired and continued in war service, returning to "civvies" in 1946. The sad task of bringing home POWs from Singapore was her last wearing Red Cross colours. Coastal work was resumed until 1956 in which year she was sold to Japan, then broken up the following year. Her dimensions were 445 ft (135 m) long and 60 ft (18 m) wide.*

The Hobart *Mercury* of 17 December 1980 reported that she was "in a dilapidated state, lying in Perama Bay near Piraeus, the port for Athens, as the Greek ship *Hellas* . . . Sold to Greek interests in 1959 for trading around their many islands, she now lies with other unwanted ships waiting for the world's economic situation to raise the price of scrap metal."

MV *Mount Newman*

EXPORTING TO THE WORLD

Shipping has continued to change through this century. The many smart coastal passenger liners such as *Taroona*, *Manunda*, *Manoora* and *Kanimbla* linked our capital cities until 1939 and then served honourably during the war as hospital ships, assault ships, troopers, etc. Built during the 1920s and 1930s, they were old ladies at the end of hostilities and were unable to compete with the railways—the newer means of passenger travel within the country. Their fate was foreign ownership or the scrap yard. Airlines today cater for overseas passenger traffic so that the elegant overseas liners, which greatly enriched our population after the war, no longer add grace and colour to our harbours. Only a few remain to go cruising.

However for an island nation ships still remain the best means of cargo transport, but here again there have been changes. To the need to ship Australia's traditional exports of wheat, wool and meat there has been added the need to find a means of shipping the country's mineral riches of coal, iron ore, alumina and so on, and to handle these products efficiently meant to ship them in bulk. To meet this change a new type of ship has evolved. Our harbours are now dominated by the oil tanker, the container ship and the bulk carrier, ranging in size from big to bigger.

Mount Newman represents an early model of the big ones of her class. 872 ft (262 m) long, 153 ft 6 ins (40.7 m) wide, 72 ft 2 ins (22.6 m) deep, drawing 53 ft 2 ins (16.2 m) fully loaded 137 475 tons (139 681 t) displacement. One powerful nine-cylinder diesel engine turns a single screw to give a service speed of 15 knots, using 72 tonnes of fuel daily. With the aid of computer controls, it requires a complement of only thirty-seven to operate this mass of ship. Accurate navigation is ensured by computer-assisted satellite systems.

Mount Newman was chartered while still under construction at the famous Belfast yards of Harland and Woolf and made her first voyage to Australia in 1973. On this voyage she took a full load of iron ore from Brazil to Japan. It was the only time she was fully loaded. On arrival in Australia she commenced her regular ten day run from Port Hedland, Western Australia, to Port Kembla, New South Wales, with iron ore for BHP. Her full capacity was not achieved on this run because of the inadequate depth of these harbours. A Pacific swell runs in at Port Kembla and a roll of a mere 3 degrees in such a big ship would increase the draught by 1 metre; this could block the harbour entrance. Skilful handling assured a useful trouble-free service for almost eight years and in 1981, when her charter was completed, she returned to her owners in the UK where she is still in service.

Dramatic changes in shape are evident in the design of *Mount Newman* and other bulk carriers. The flat transom stern has replaced the graceful counter stern which served to lift smaller ships over a following sea; sheer bulk has eliminated that problem. The effect of the bulbous bow is to break the bow wave smoothly, reducing the aerated seas near the stern and providing a better grip on the water for the screw and rudder. This minimises fuel consumption. The bridge—a ship's head office—and all personnel occupy a towering structure aft with the engines

MV MOUNT NEWMAN

immediately beneath, leaving a clear money-earning cargo space. Economy has been the designer's aim; "cost effectiveness" their new by-word.

Now even bigger vessels are in the bulk trade, longer and wider but of less draught to suit our harbours. One of these is BHP's own *Iron Newcastle*. On her maiden voyage in January 1986 she loaded 133 471 tonnes of iron ore at Port Hedland. This she discharged at Port Kembla and Newcastle, and after a quick loading of 135 000 tonnes of coal she was on her way to Japan within two days. Her crew totals twenty-six. At the beginning of the twentieth century such a task would have involved about forty-five average sized ships, each requiring a full week's loading time, with crews totalling about 1350 men.

"Containerisation" is another word new in our language; it simply means carrying the cargo packed in boxes. These are big boxes designed for little handling, and to fit in with railway and road services—as motorists often notice on our highways. There are refrigerated boxes for meat and other perishables, boxes for machinery parts, boxes for everything. These are stored in the hold and, being weatherproof, on the deck. While the mundane box is the modern cargo carrier the ship which transports it is still an impessive sight, to some a stirring one that is imbued with the romance that the sea conveys to all who sail her oceans.

The bulk carrier while not a new idea has evolved over many years. James Cook's little *Endeavour* was a collier and many small ships since have plied our coastline with coal, timber, wheat and similar cargoes. Today's changing conditions have produced the highy specialised big bulk carrier and the big container ship with its equally specialised wharfside cargo-handling equipment, termed the "container terminal".

Shipping is now a complex, big business affair. The great little men of the last century might well gape with amazement at what has grown from their efforts. Among the newer developments is a combination of container and bulk carrier, the TNT *Express*, Australian-manned but British-registered. Australia depends on its sea links just as much today as it did in 1788. The Australian flag is carried across all the oceans by Broken Hill Proprietary Company Limited and the Australian National Line.

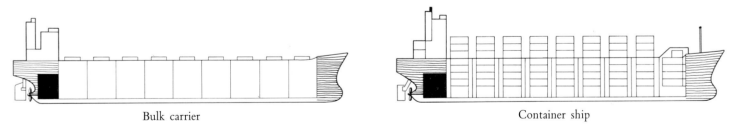

Bulk carrier   Container ship

Cut-away views of a bulk carrier and container ship show the ratio of engine space to paying space in each.

⚓ *Mount Newman* is shown in the old ANL funnel colours. The powerful tugs assisting in the docking manoeuvre are dwarfed alongside her massive hull.

Australia II

NATIONAL PRIDE HAS A HEYDAY

The romance and beauty of sail did not fade with the domination of engine power on the world sea routes. Sail continued to combine beauty and pleasure, satisfying the aesthetic needs of human nature. It provided relaxation and excitement, the seductive feeling of sliding silently across a calm sea and the exhilaration of a tussle with wind and water. The yacht offered a whole gamut of sensation in a more pleasurable manner than in the old square-rigger days. All this brought sailing a new status.

There is hardly any similarity between the stately old sailing ships that blew across oceans and the modern yacht, except that both deal with the same elements. There were boats built purely for pleasure centuries ago, but the yacht of today evolved from the fishing boats and other utilitarian craft of the last 150 years.

The schooner *America*, winner of the cup that bears her name, was derived from the Sandy Hook pilot boat; the English yachts she vanquished in 1851 were a version of the old Customs Revenue cutters. Today's racer is a highly specialised craft, far removed from its predecessors even though its power still comes from the wind.

The heavy cotton canvas of the old-timer has given way to lightweight synthetic sailcloth, Mylar, so smooth and thin as to be translucent. This is reinforced in the area of greatest strain by sections of Kevlar, which, in addition to having enormous strength, maintains the sail's aerodynamic shape, enabling it to use the wind's power more effectively. The stainless steel standing rigging holding up the tall hollow aluminium mast is so thin and light as to be almost invisible.

Another contrast can be seen in the hull, which is now made of lightweight structural material and has distinctive contours with long overhangs at bow and stern and a short but deep keel, to quicken manoeuvrability. It is fitted with a variety of winches and a range of wind-reading and other instruments that would bewilder the sailormen of the old *America* and even yachtsmen of as recent a time as thirty years ago. Competition has made today's crack racing yachts almost equally equipped technologically, although the skill of the sailors still remains the winning factor. Tactics in placing the boat in an advantageous position and using the wind efficiently may be assisted by the array of instruments, but the skipper and his crew make and carry out the decisions on which winning depends.

Australia's love of sport is widely recognised and in sailing we've had our fair share of success. Honours have been won at the Olympic Games, in the Admiral's Cup and in the many other international races held for individual

The painting shows Australia II *flying a shy spinnaker with a light jib set inside on a forestay to catch any wind the other sails may miss. She is set against the sun to show the light translucent fabric of her racing sails; the darker area of her mainsail is the stronger Kevlar section.*

Yacht *AUSTRALIA II*

classes of yachts. But yachting's most prestigious international event, the America's Cup, eluded us through six attempts over thirty years. It had been held in America for 132 years, surviving twenty-four international challenges. The twenty-fifth brought the trophy to Australia.

The proud moment when, after a tense series of races off Newport, USA, *Australia II* crossed the line to complete a 4–3 score was watched worldwide on television. It put Australia on the map as much as the Portuguese, Dutch, French and British navigators had centuries earlier.

Australia II is still at home with us. Her aluminium hull is 19.5 m long overall, 13.8 m on the waterline and 3.7 m wide, and draws 2.7 m. Her mast reaches 25 m above the deck and she has quite a wardrobe of sails for every occasion. In many respects she differs little technologically from her rivals, except for the famous "winged keel". This, simply stated, has the effect of providing a better grip on the sea when she is heeling with the wind.

That simple feature was an Australian idea developed in testing tank research conducted in Holland, while sail fabrics and materials were the result of other overseas technological research—all of which indicates clearly enough that we are no longer isolated from the rest of the world. But the team of designers, crew and sponsors were all Australians.

American pilot schooner.
The first America's Cup winner was based on this yacht.

British Customs Revenue cutter.
This design formed the basis for English yachts of the mid-nineteenth century.